Chris Wendel
3rd Period
English
Nov, 2013

Assignment: Write a Poem

I can feel the heat underfoot.
My soles are thinning beneath.
As voices call from down below,
I shed my

Chris,
If you couldn't complete
the assignment, you
should have asked for
help.

And what happened to your paper??!?!?!?!

Unfinished

Cover Design by: Chris Wendel

Cover Photo by: Intergalactic Design Studio /
http://www.istockphoto.com/user_view.php?id=333920

Other Photo Credits belong to:

Retrovizor / http://www.istockphoto.com/user_view.php?id=2583833

Jmbatt / http://www.istockphoto.com/user_view.php?id=2103578

TopshotUK / http://www.istockphoto.com/user_view.php?id=1054943

MissPig / http://www.istockphoto.com/user_view.php?id=3207772

Giacoff / http://www.istockphoto.com/user_view.php?id=398267

Risus / http://www.istockphoto.com/user_view.php?id=4632052

ISBN: 978-0-9895714-4-9
e-ISBN: 978-0-9895714-5-6

HP

HOLDEN PUBLISHING

ALL   BOOKS   BY   CHRIS   WENDEL

NOVELS

Human After All

(Introducing Det. Tom Gray and Valerie Hardy)

SHORT STORIES

Human After All: The Pen Pal Chronicle

(An Amazon Bestseller)

BUSINESS BOOKS

Converting Customers to Clients

On Strengthening Business Relationships

POEMS

Unfinished

UPCOMING NOVEL

King of Pain

(A Det. Tom Gray Novel)

Introduction

Throughout the course of the last year, a very trying time for me personally, I wrote many two to 10 lines of a text in poem/lyric style, and I never went back to complete them. I knew at the time these lines of text were simply my way of dealing with the many emotions I had during a life-changing year. However, when my life and world had settled, I began wondering how I would complete these poems/lyrics. How would I reconnect with that moment when they were first written down? Did I want to reconnect with that moment?

I realized these poems could have a thousand different endings, just like life. With that realization I figured out what I wanted to do with these poems.

I am submitting the contents of this book to you. Close the poems/lyrics however you see fit. The pages herein are designed for you to write in the book. If you play an instrument, set the poems/lyrics to music. Give these texts titles. Give them life—a life I could never dream to give them.

All I ask is you take a picture of the final product you create and email it to me or upload it to my Facebook or Twitter feeds. If you create a song with them, video it or record it. Email me, add it to my feeds as well. Just give us both writing credit. Let's create something together. Whatever you do with it, just get it to me. I'd like to share them with the world.

Together we can write any ending we want.

Enjoy!

-- CW

DEDICATION

To Holden Wendel

Your life is your greatest story.

Enjoy the thrill of making any ending of it you like.

ACKNOWLEDGEMENTS

Michelle Bonnin

Thank you for being the best part of a new beginning.

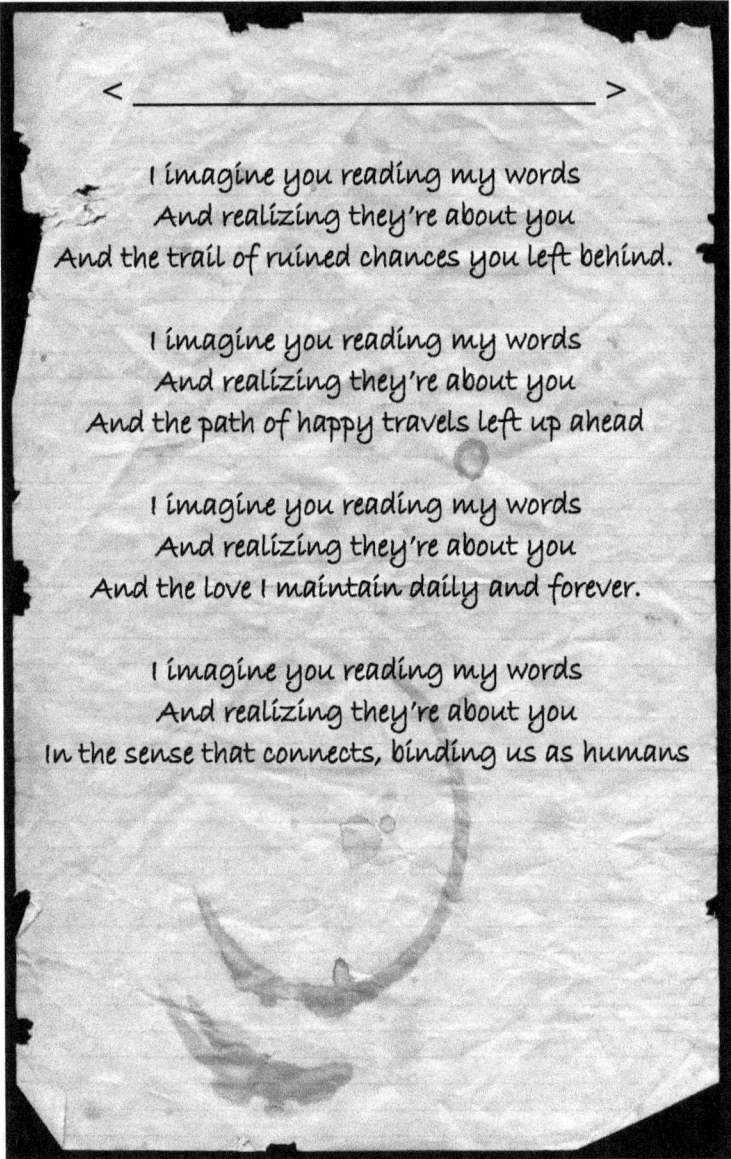

< —————————————————— >

I imagine you reading my words
And realizing they're about you
And the trail of ruined chances you left behind.

I imagine you reading my words
And realizing they're about you
And the path of happy travels left up ahead

I imagine you reading my words
And realizing they're about you
And the love I maintain daily and forever.

I imagine you reading my words
And realizing they're about you
In the sense that connects, binding us as humans

< _____ >

I can feel the heat underfoot.
My soles are thinning beneath.
As voices call from down below,
I shed my skin to bequeath.

Sirens sing of haunted decades,
While souls lost kill the sentry.
Aboleths prey darkened waters,
Waiting for human entry.

Where can I roam for safe haven?
Free from belkers in the fog?
I just need some place peaceful now.
Protecting goodness I slog.

<   >

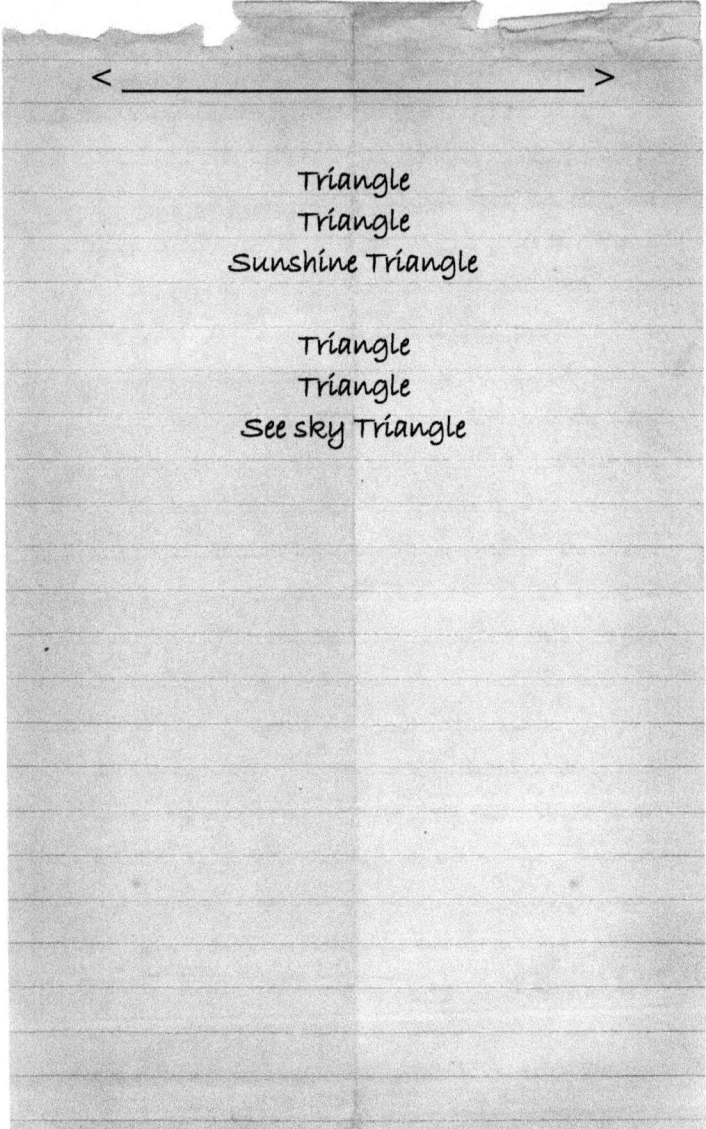

Triangle
Triangle
Sunshine Triangle

Triangle
Triangle
See sky Triangle

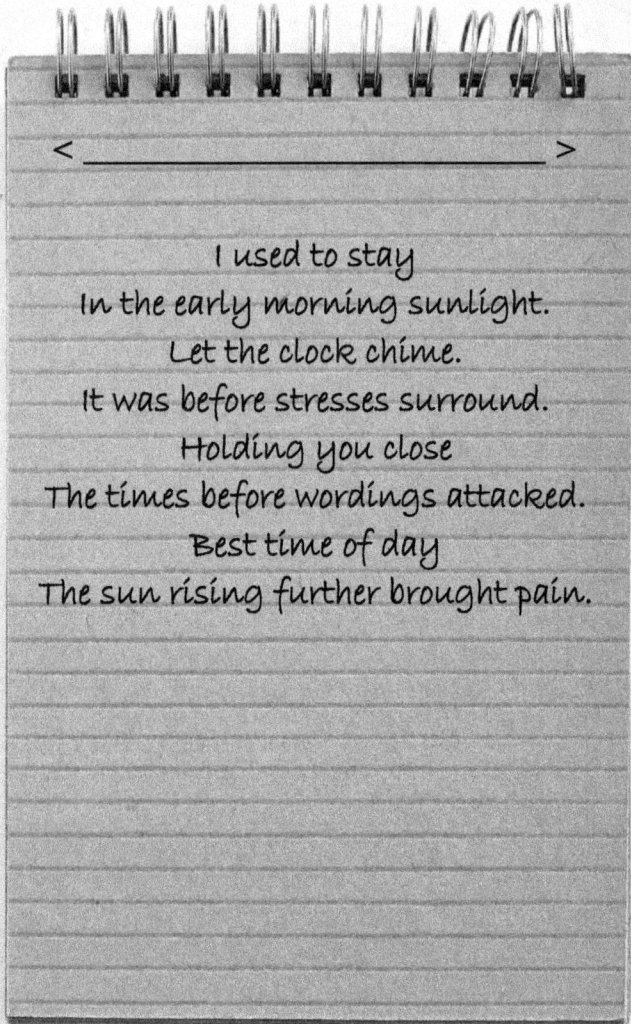

I used to stay
In the early morning sunlight.
Let the clock chime.
It was before stresses surround.
Holding you close
The times before wordings attacked.
Best time of day
The sun rising further brought pain.

Leave it in the past;
Don't ruin now.
Leave it in the past;
Tomorrow comes.
Leave it in the past;
Sun shines somehow.
Leave it in the past;
Let it run numb.
Leave it in the past;

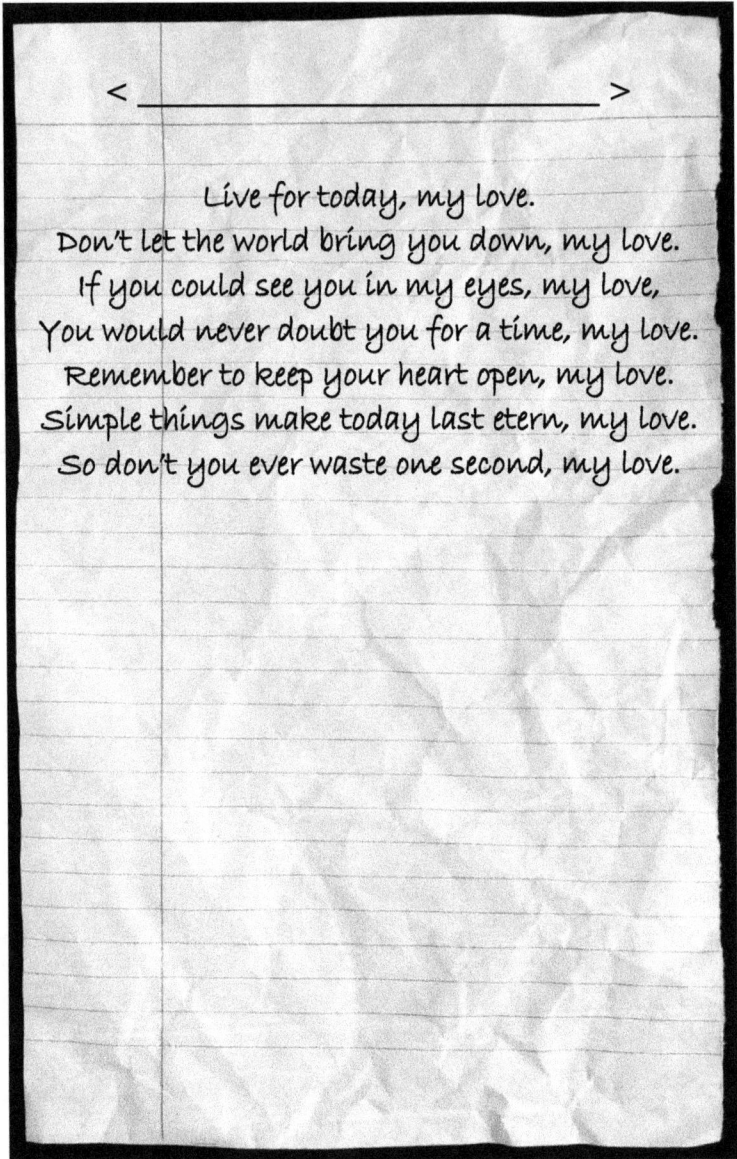

<
_____
>

Live for today, my love.
Don't let the world bring you down, my love.
If you could see you in my eyes, my love,
You would never doubt you for a time, my love.
Remember to keep your heart open, my love.
Simple things make today last etern, my love.
So don't you ever waste one second, my love.

< _____ >

The stranger travels on,
Wearing the mask of running away.
Everyone carries on,
Racing toward what they think they want.
Connecting takes a seat
Behind moments of self-indulgence.
Narcissist perfection
Always leaves you empty and alone.
Try to let go of fear.
Expand yourself and stop judging all.

< ————————————————————— >

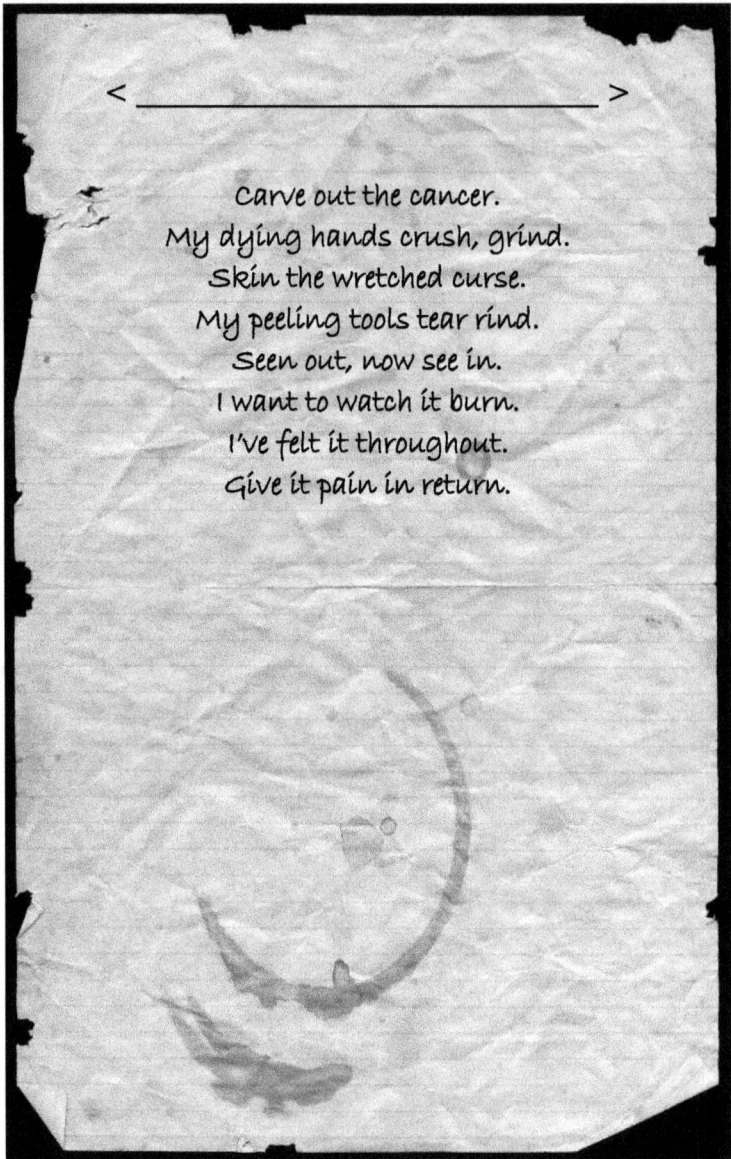

Carve out the cancer.
My dying hands crush, grind.
Skin the wretched curse.
My peeling tools tear rind.
Seen out, now see in.
I want to watch it burn.
I've felt it throughout.
Give it pain in return.

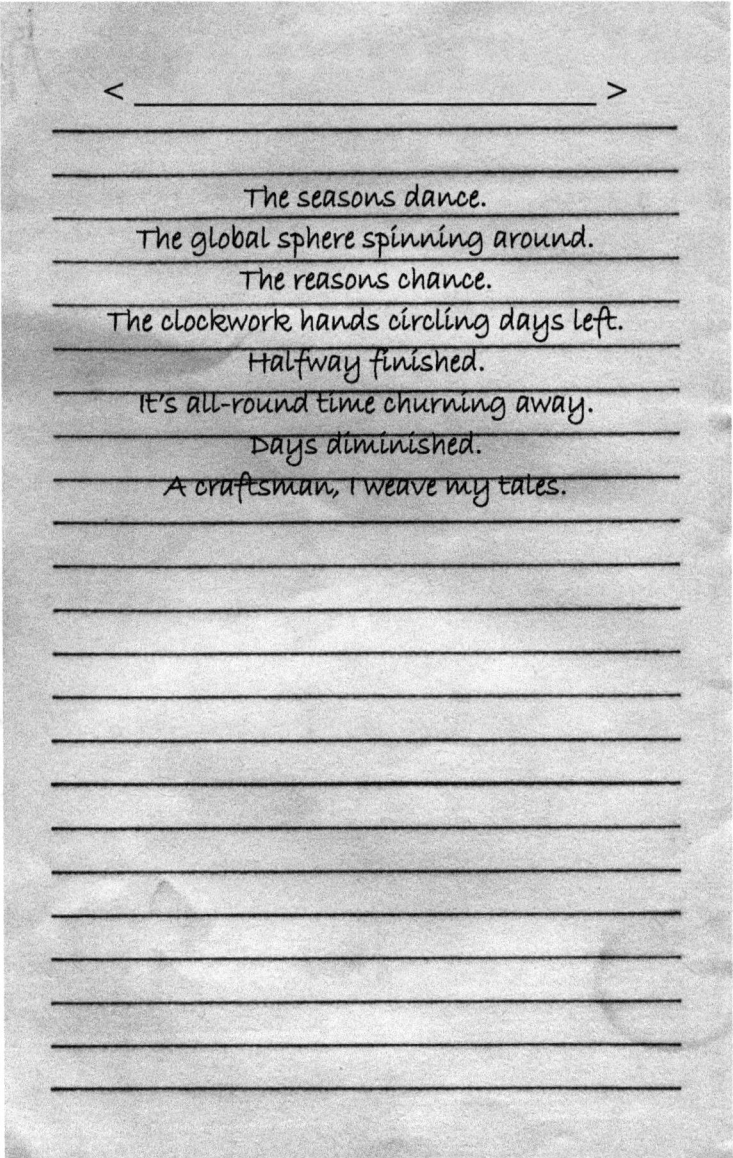

< _____ >

The seasons dance.
The global sphere spinning around.
The reasons chance.
The clockwork hands circling days left.
Halfway finished.
It's all-round time churning away.
Days diminished.
A craftsman, I weave my tales.

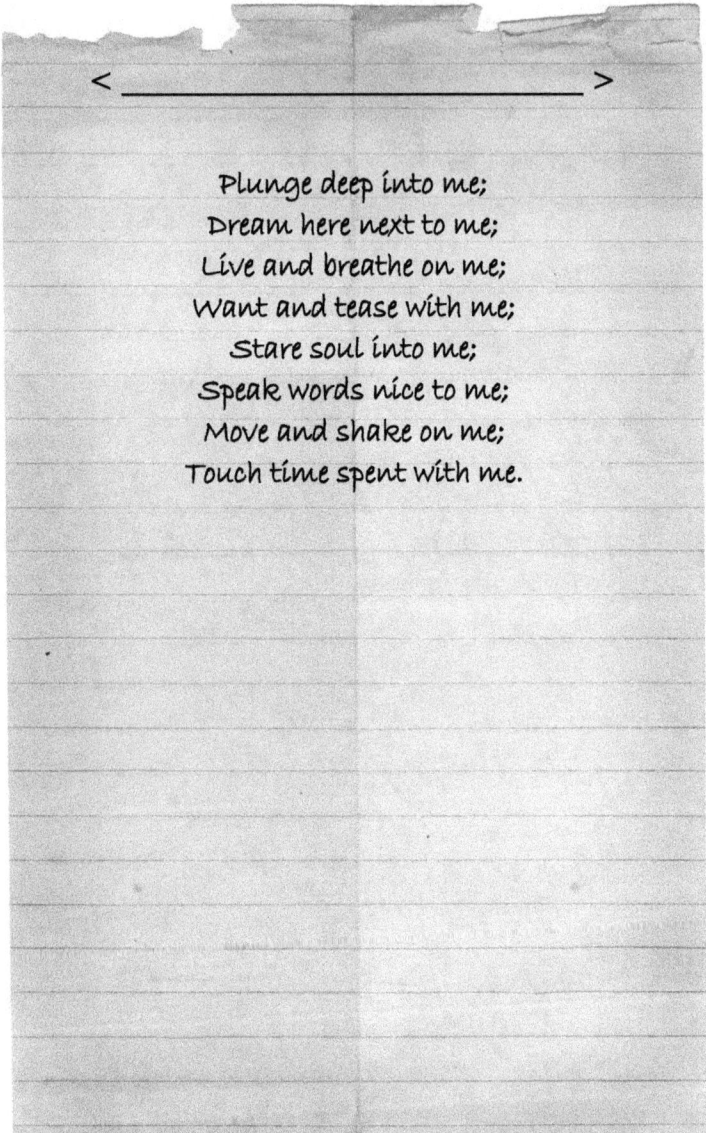

Plunge deep into me;
Dream here next to me;
Live and breathe on me;
Want and tease with me;
Stare soul into me;
Speak words nice to me;
Move and shake on me;
Touch time spent with me.

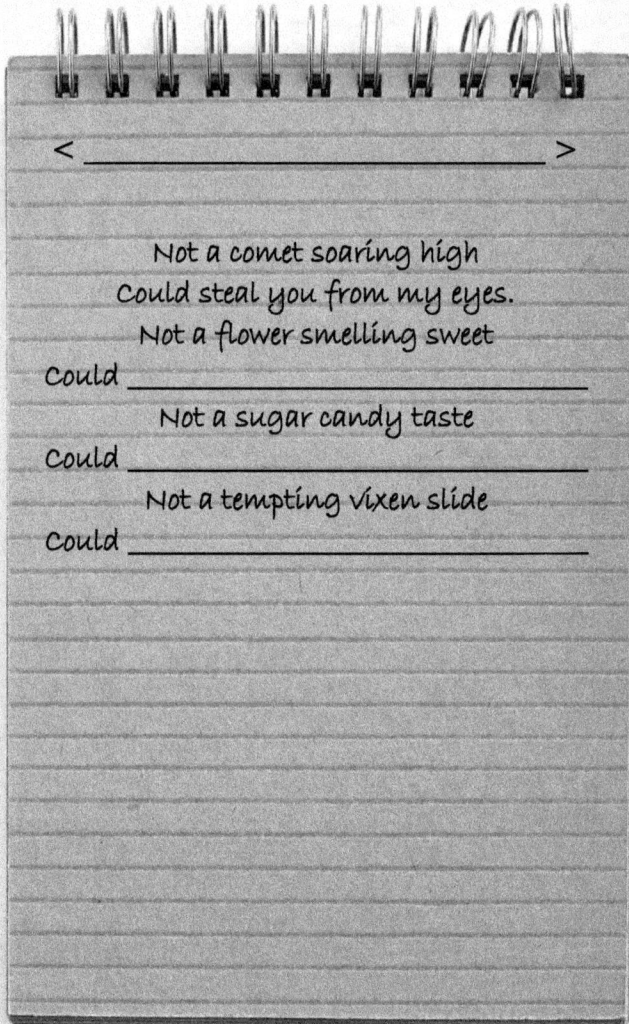

< _____ >

Not a comet soaring high
Could steal you from my eyes.
Not a flower smelling sweet
Could _____

Not a sugar candy taste
Could _____

Not a tempting vixen slide
Could _____

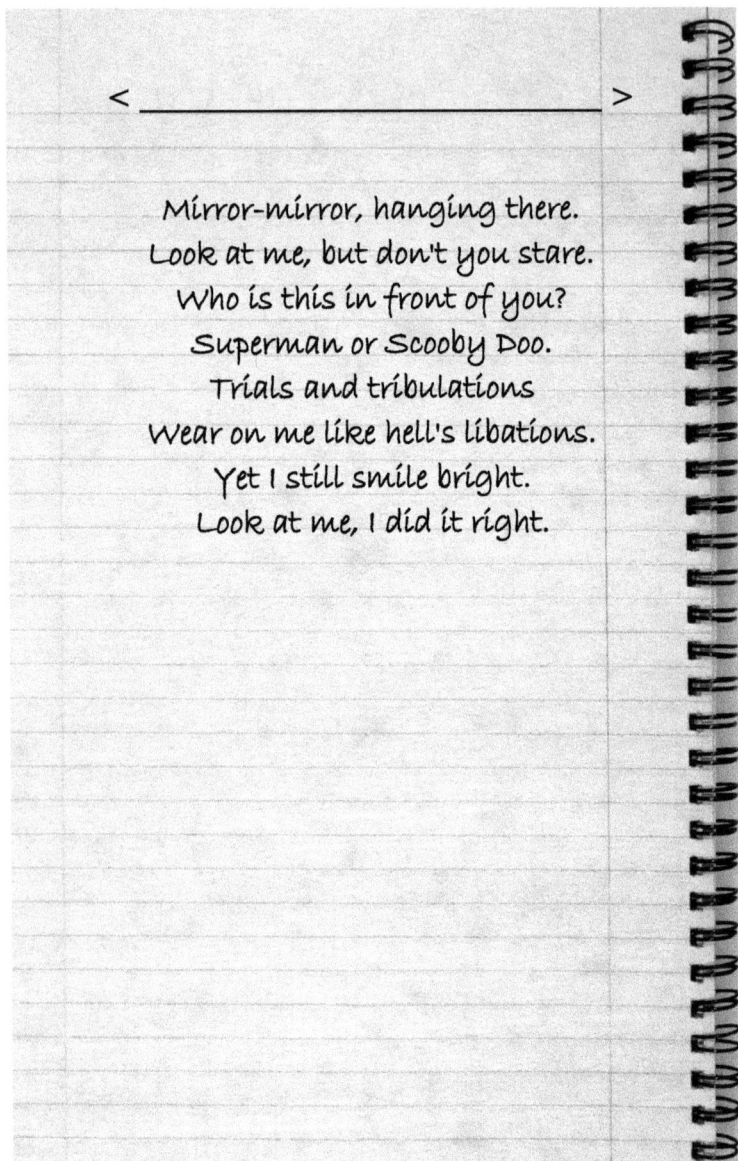

Mirror-mirror, hanging there.
Look at me, but don't you stare.
Who is this in front of you?
Superman or Scooby Doo.
Trials and tribulations
Wear on me like hell's libations.
Yet I still smile bright.
Look at me, I did it right.

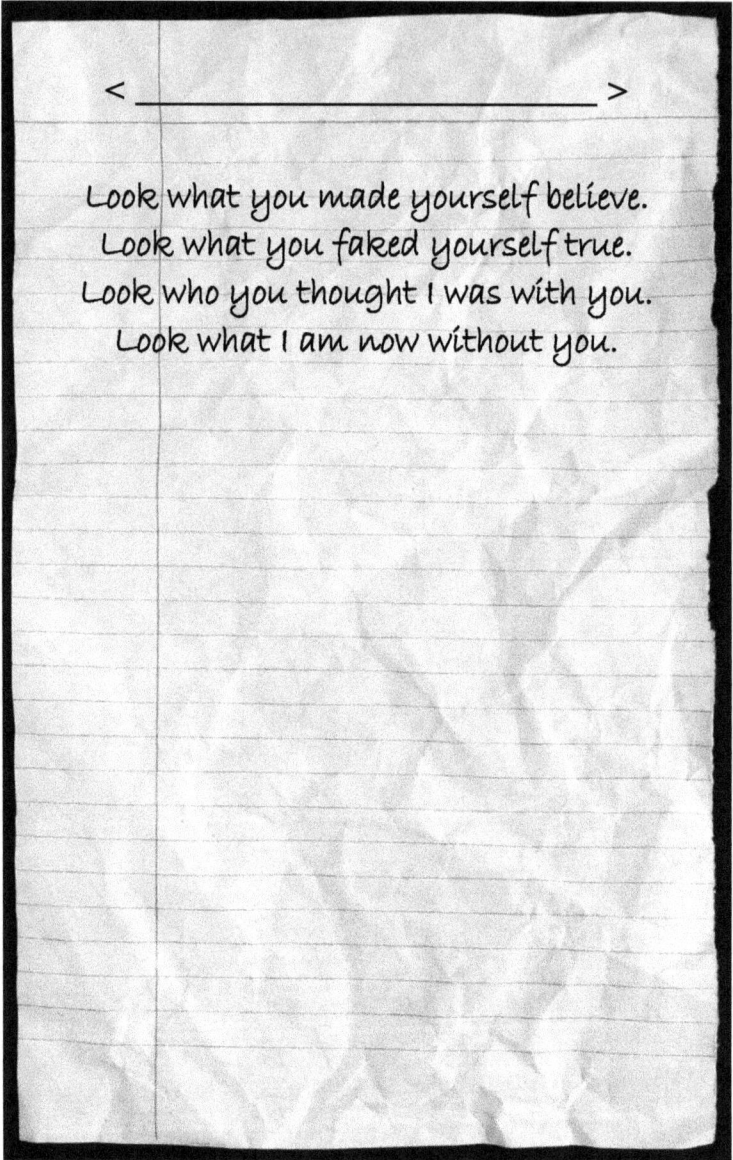

Look what you made yourself believe.
Look what you faked yourself true.
Look who you thought I was with you.
Look what I am now without you.

< _____ >

Could've done without her judgments.
Could've done without her lies.
Could've done without her cheating.
Could've done without her pain.
Could've done without her.
I enjoy laughing again.
I am feeling like myself.
So thank you for that smile.
Thank out for that joy.

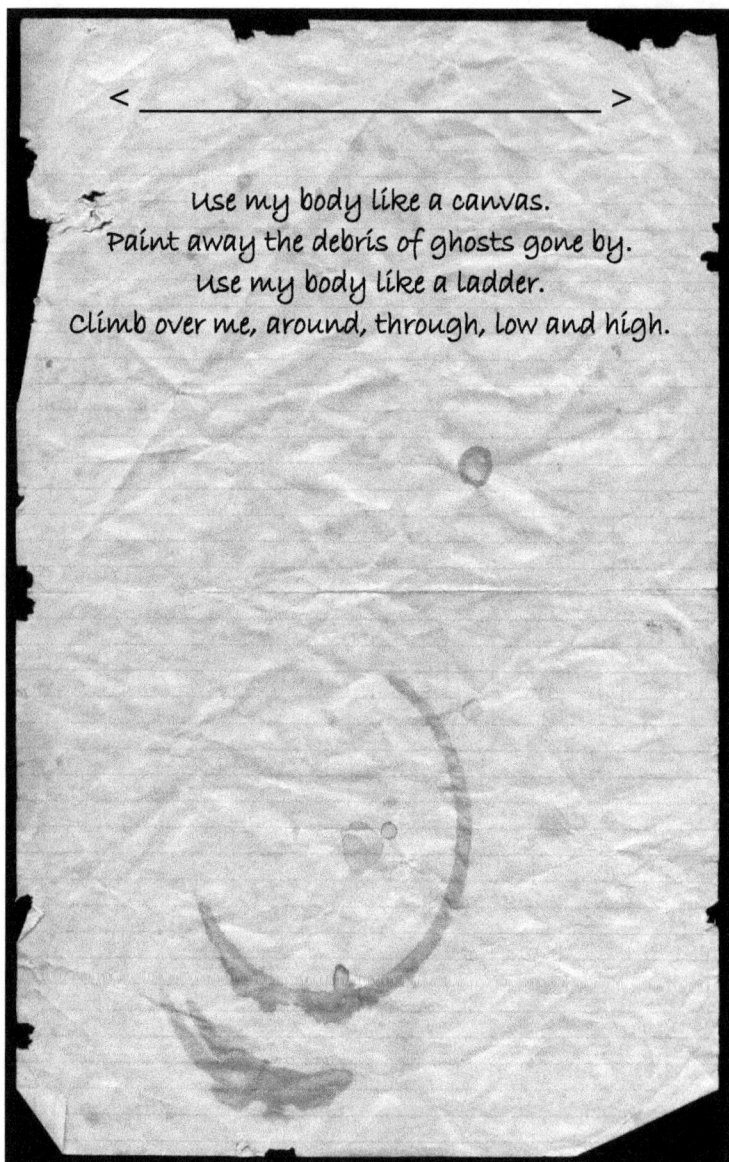

< ——————————— >

Use my body like a canvas.
Paint away the debris of ghosts gone by.
Use my body like a ladder.
Climb over me, around, through, low and high.

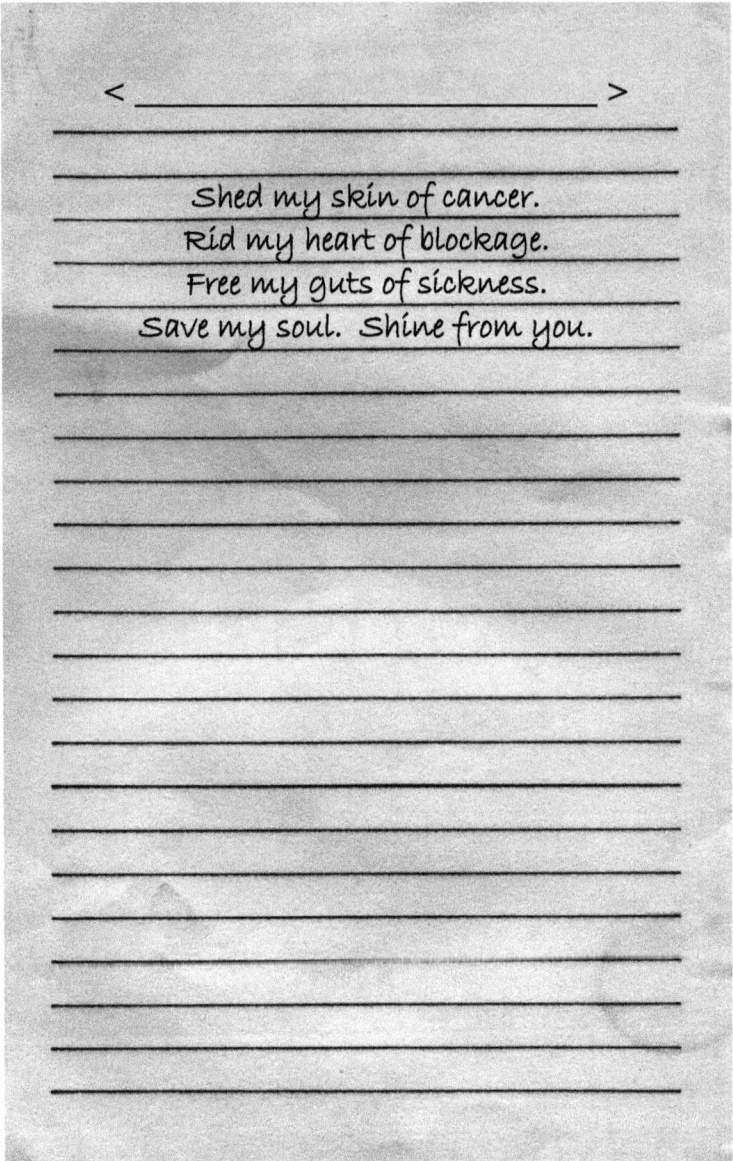

< _____ >

Shed my skin of cancer.
Rid my heart of blockage.
Free my guts of sickness.
Save my soul. Shine from you.

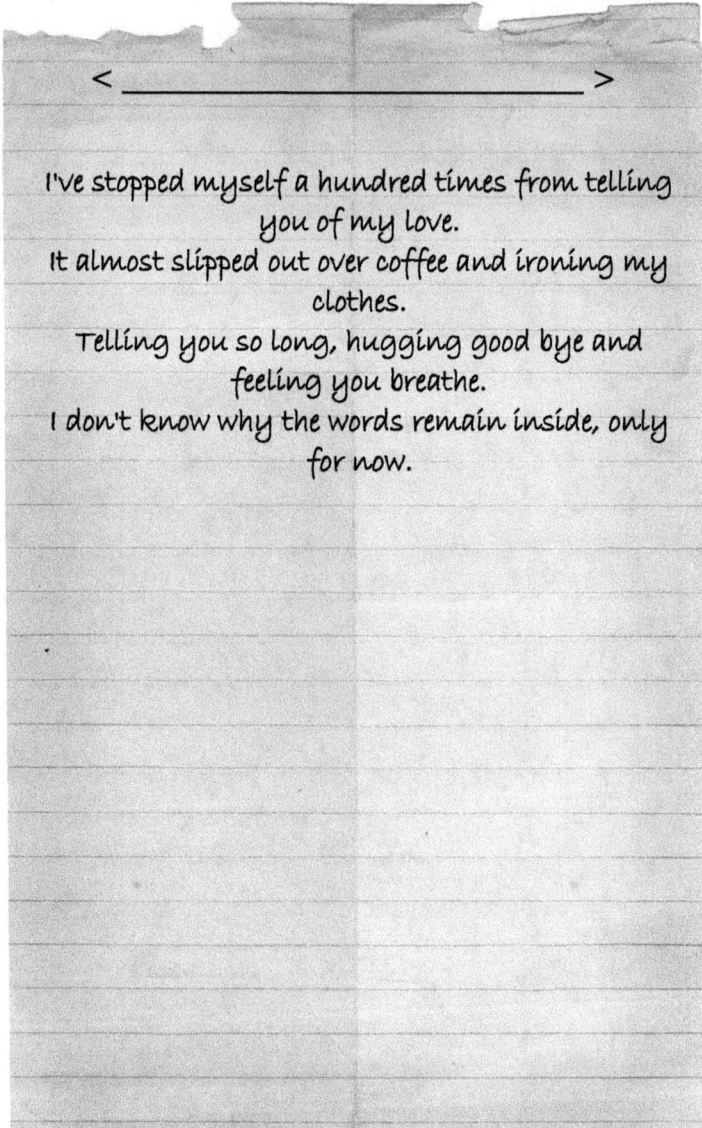

< _____ >

I've stopped myself a hundred times from telling
you of my love.
It almost slipped out over coffee and ironing my
clothes.
Telling you so long, hugging good bye and
feeling you breathe.
I don't know why the words remain inside, only
for now.

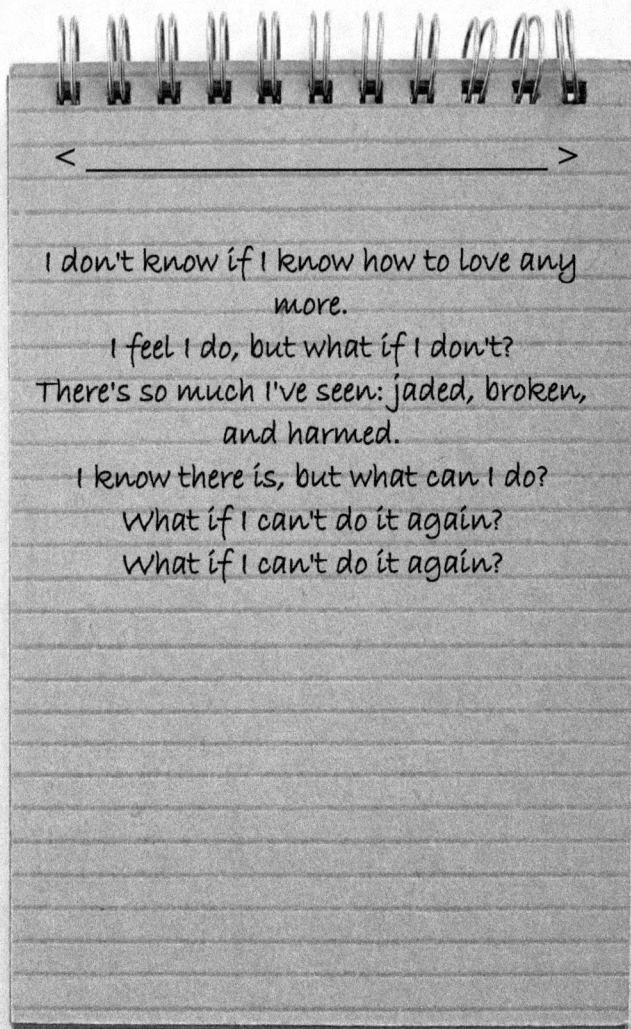

< _____ >

I don't know if I know how to love any
more.
I feel I do, but what if I don't?
There's so much I've seen: jaded, broken,
and harmed.
I know there is, but what can I do?
What if I can't do it again?
What if I can't do it again?

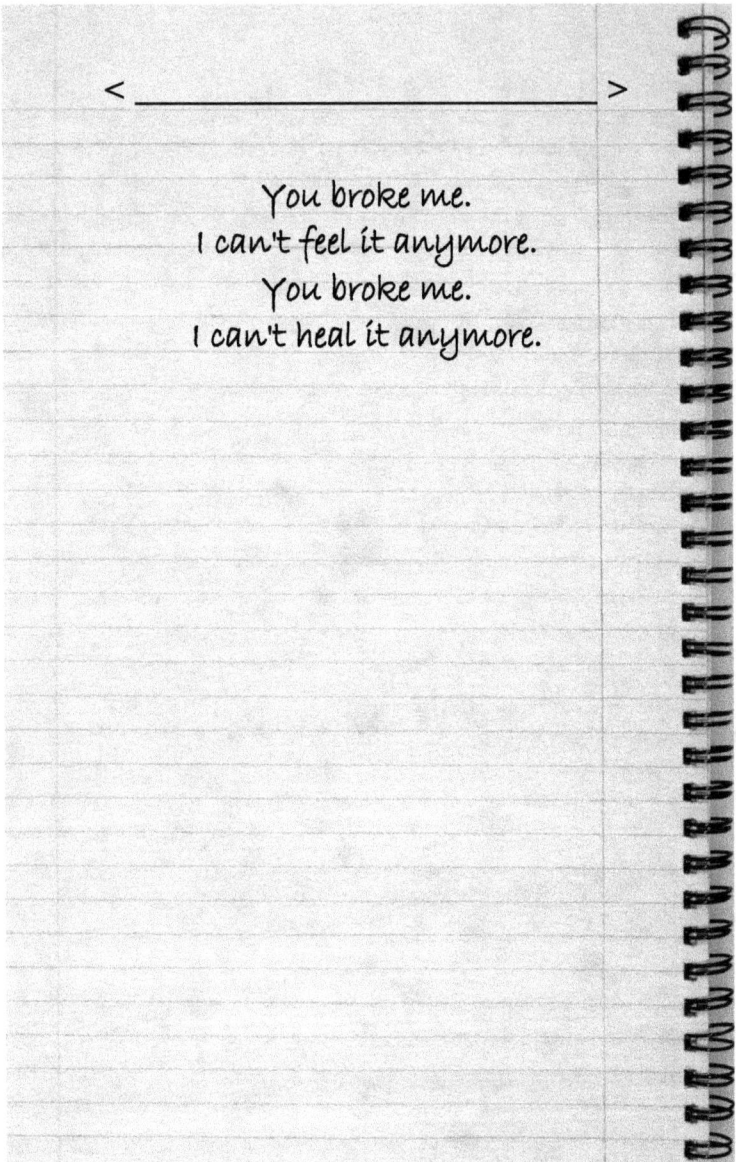

< _____ >

You broke me.
I can't feel it anymore.
You broke me.
I can't heal it anymore.

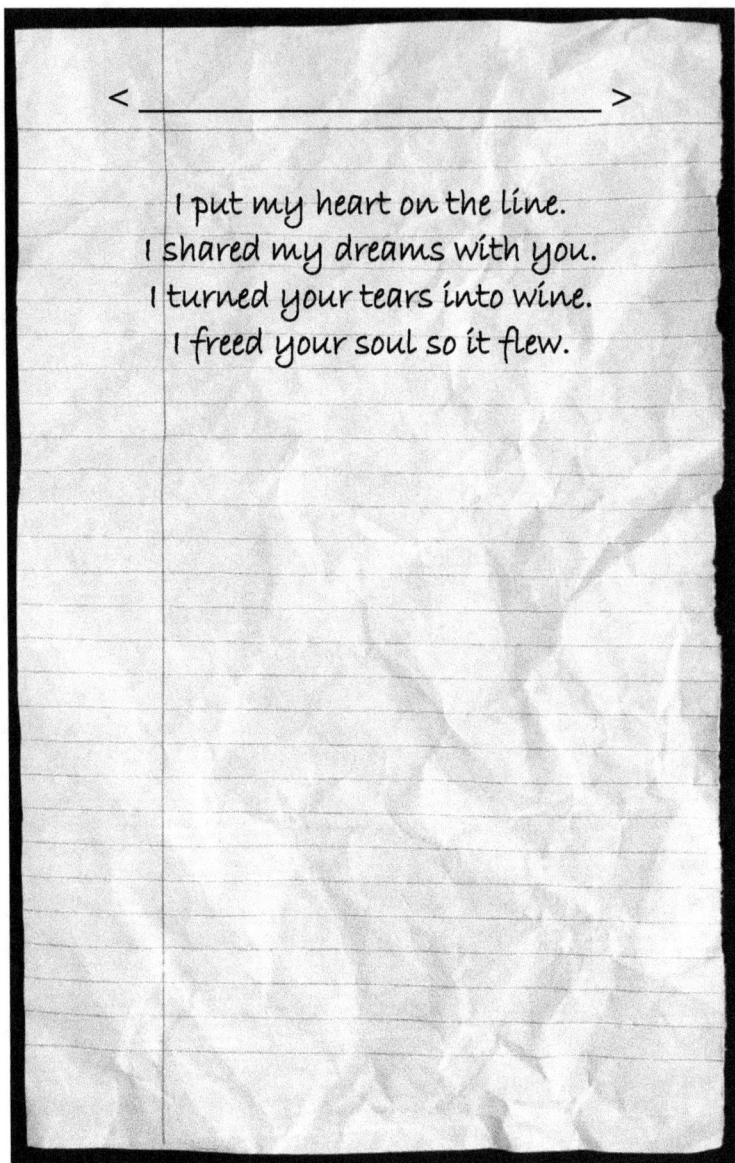

< _____ >

I put my heart on the line.
I shared my dreams with you.
I turned your tears into wine.
I freed your soul so it flew.

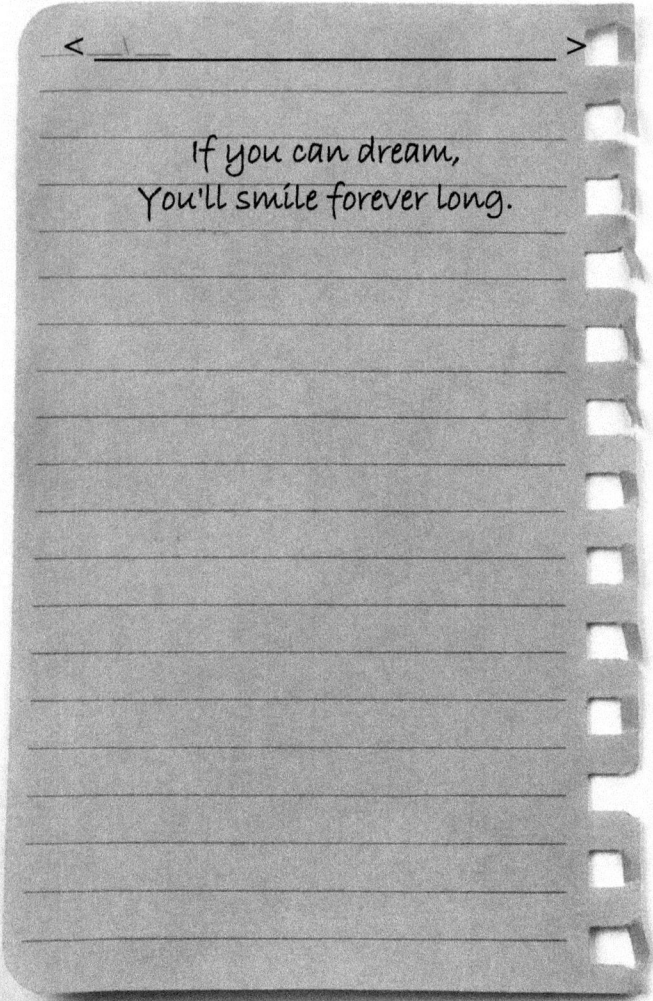

If you can dream,
You'll smile forever long.

< ———————————————— >

I saw your picture today,
And you looked so sad.
Looks like your soul flew away,
And nothing's there you had.
Well I'm not sorry to say
That it makes me feel glad.

I hope your ev'nings are cold.

I hope your dreams all feel sold.

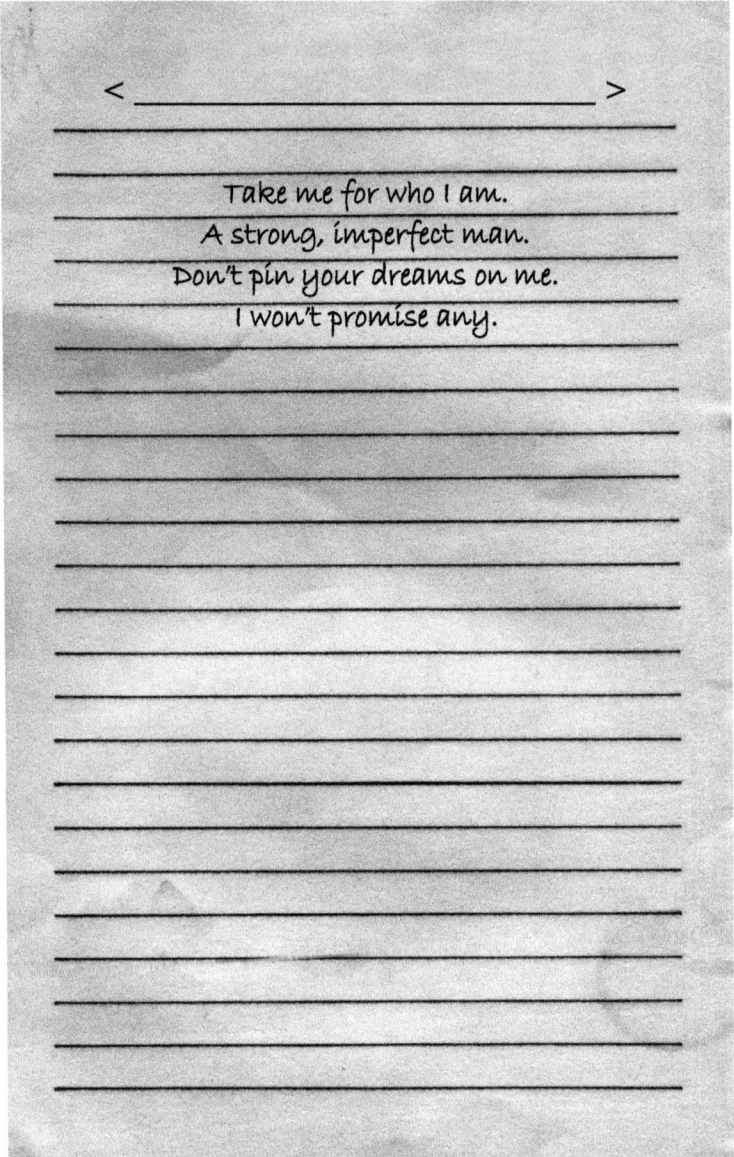

Take me for who I am.
A strong, imperfect man.
Don't pin your dreams on me.
I won't promise any.

< _____ >

Leaving pieces of me behind
Like a bread crumb trail of who I've been.
Turning to face what used to be.
Boy, I sure like where I'm laying right now.

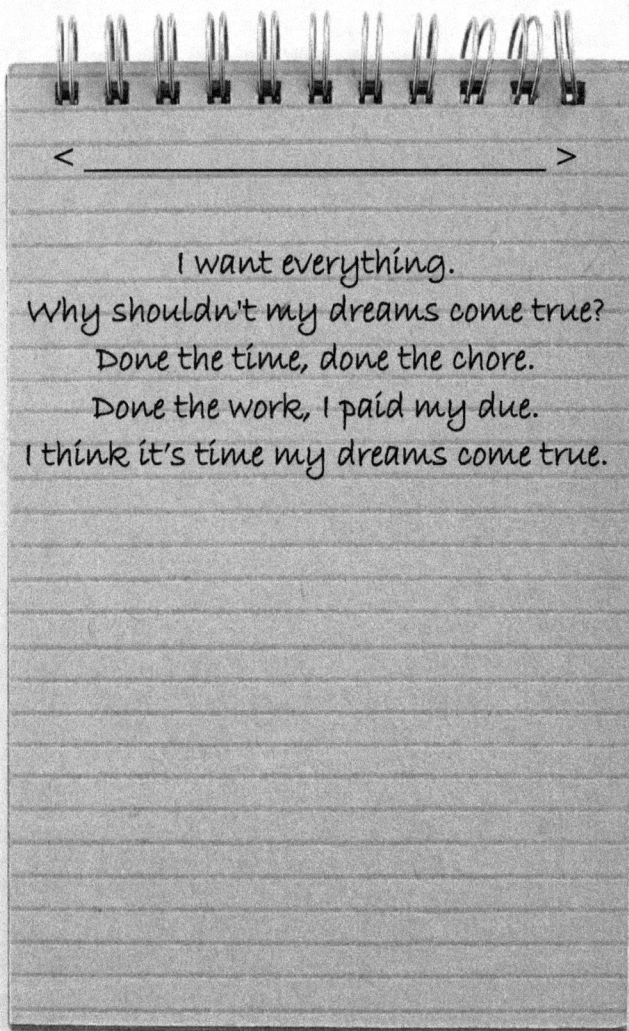

I want everything.
Why shouldn't my dreams come true?
Done the time, done the chore.
Done the work, I paid my due.
I think it's time my dreams come true.

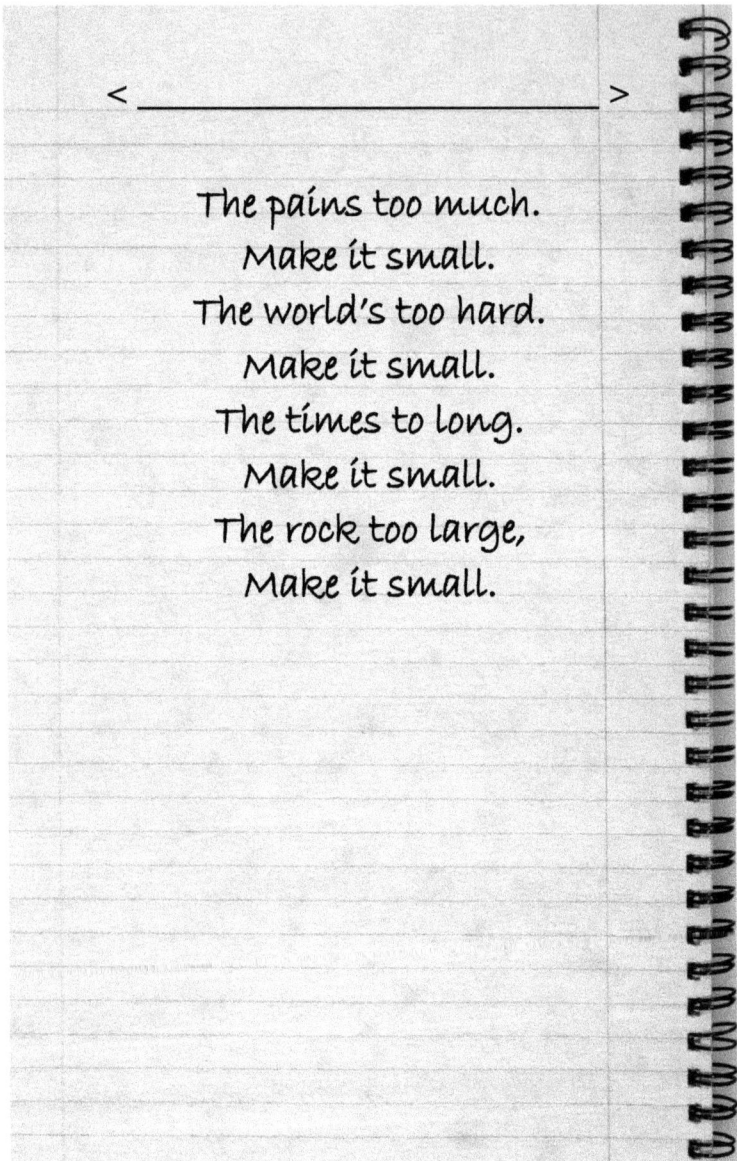

<

>

The pains too much.
Make it small.
The world's too hard.
Make it small.
The times to long.
Make it small.
The rock too large,
Make it small.

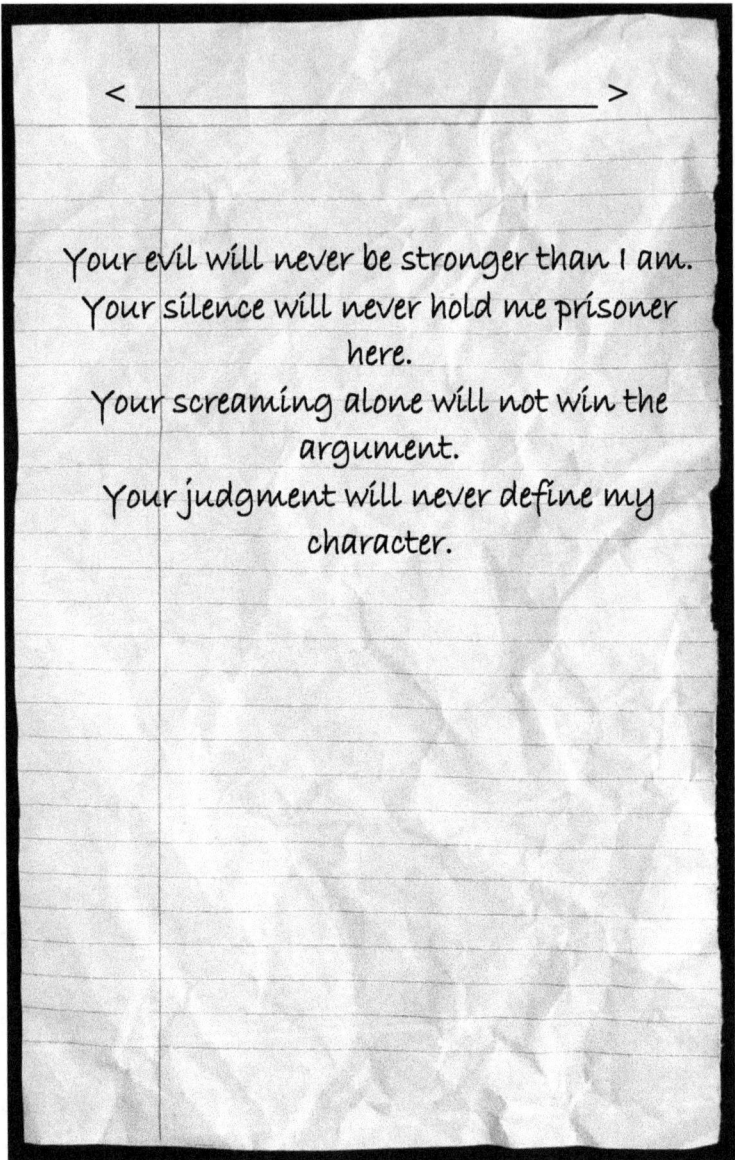

Your evil will never be stronger than I am.
Your silence will never hold me prisoner here.
Your screaming alone will not win the argument.
Your judgment will never define my character.

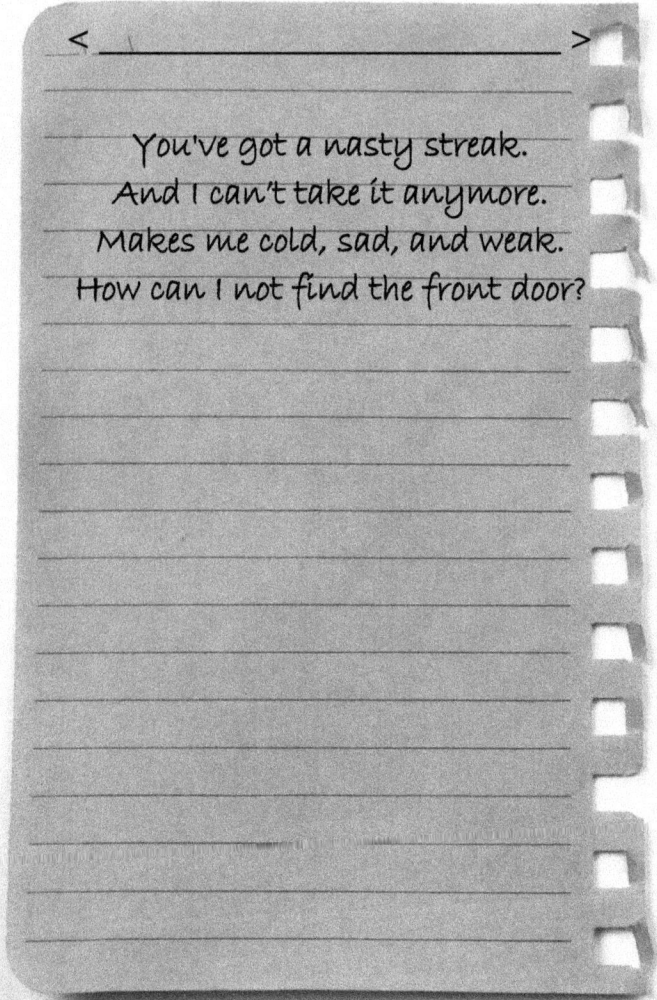

You've got a nasty streak.
And I can't take it anymore.
Makes me cold, sad, and weak.
How can I not find the front door?

< ———————————————————— >

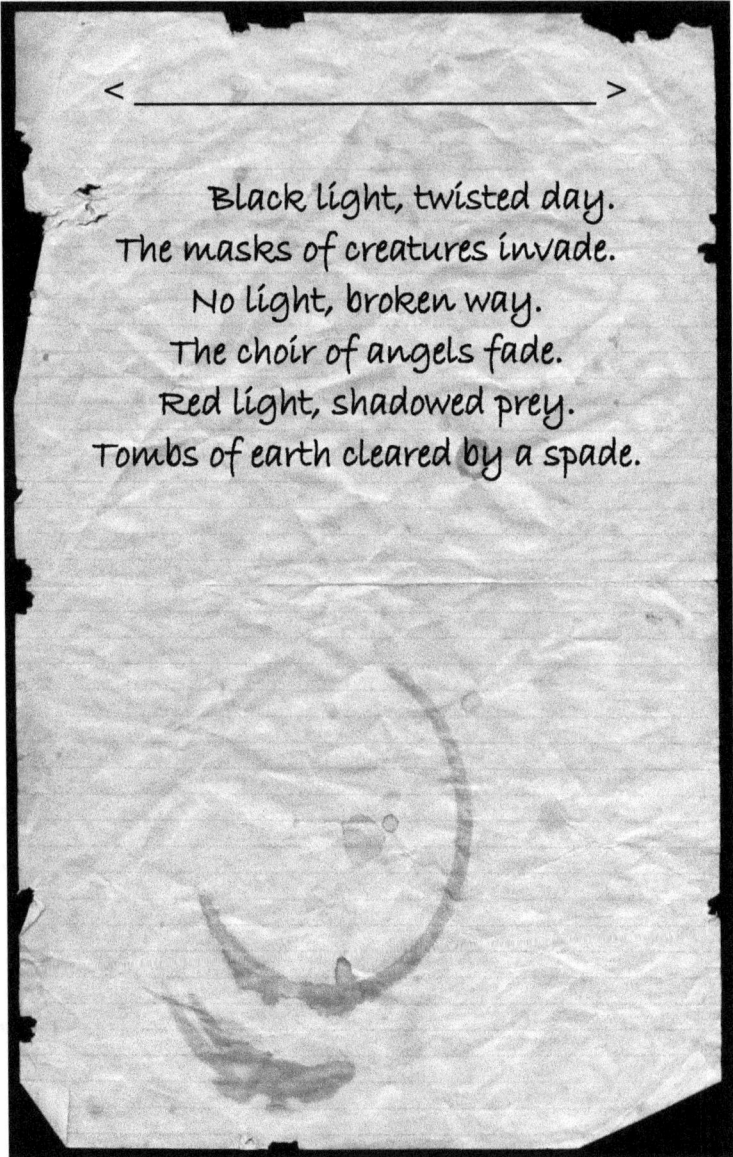

Black light, twisted day.
The masks of creatures invade.
No light, broken way.
The choir of angels fade.
Red light, shadowed prey.
Tombs of earth cleared by a spade.

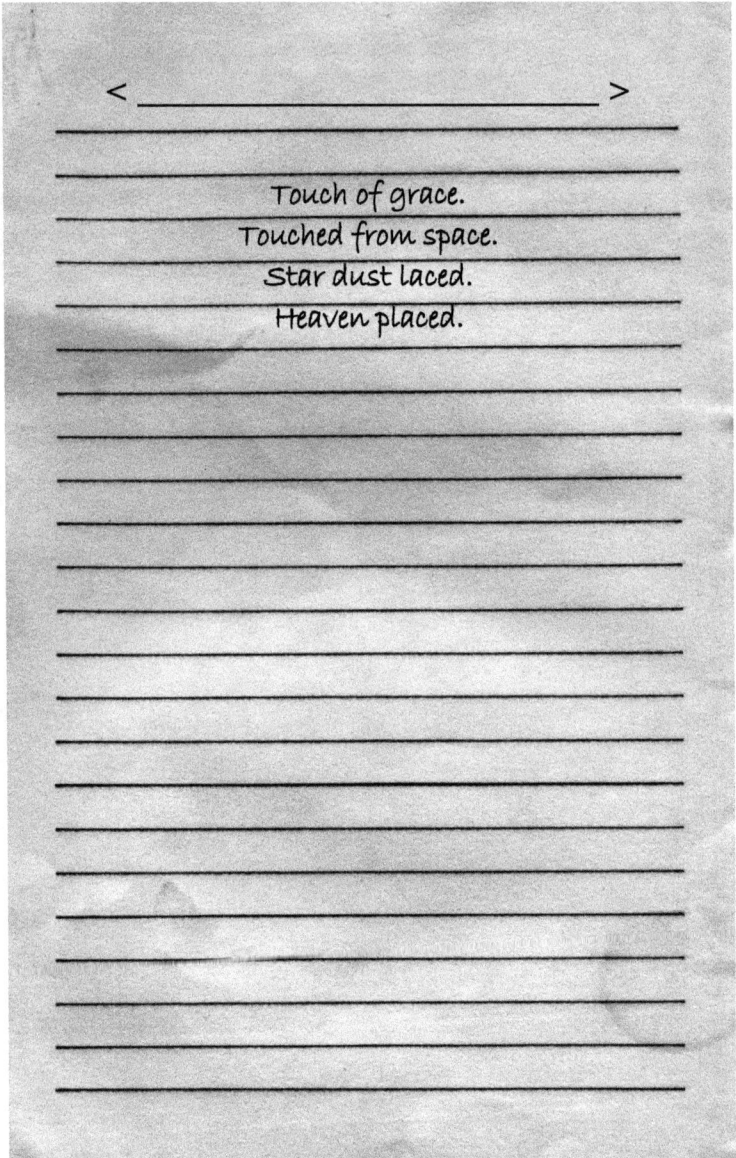

Touch of grace.
Touched from space.
Star dust laced.
Heaven placed.

< _____ >

I want to be a better man.
I want to know there's good in me.
Yet I want to live on the edge.
Boredom to be my enemy.
I want to write the best novel.
I want to see my name in lights.
Yet I want to live the best tale.
Live stories of loves, highs, and fights.

< ————————————————————— >

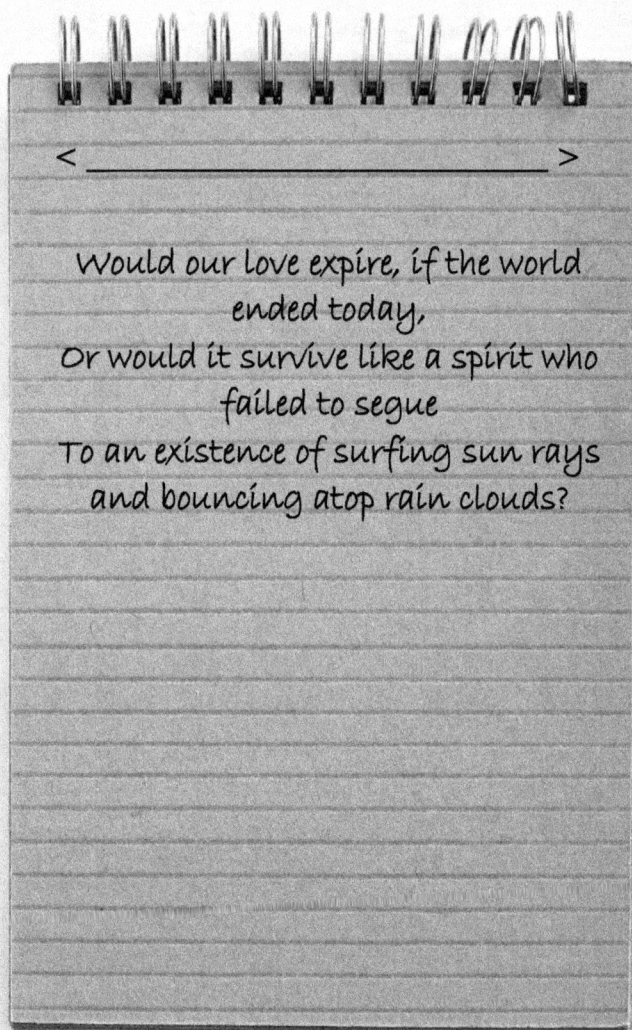

Would our love expire, if the world
ended today,
Or would it survive like a spirit who
failed to segue
To an existence of surfing sun rays
and bouncing atop rain clouds?

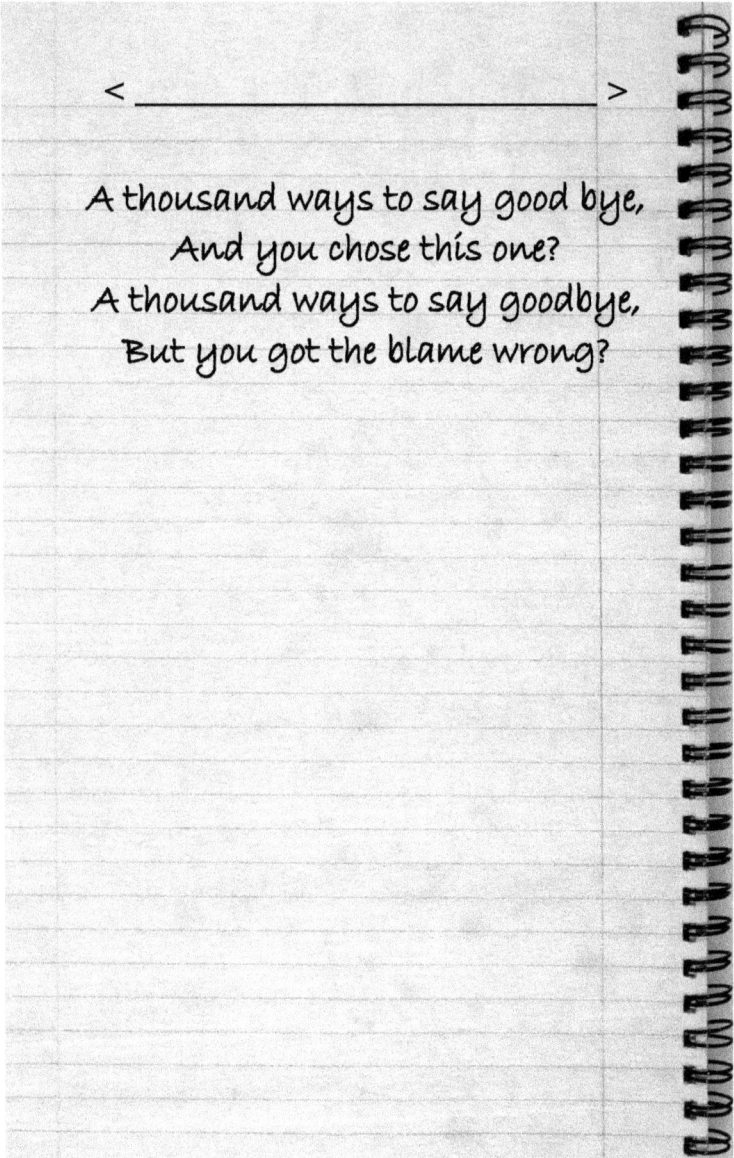

A thousand ways to say good bye,
And you chose this one?
A thousand ways to say goodbye,
But you got the blame wrong?

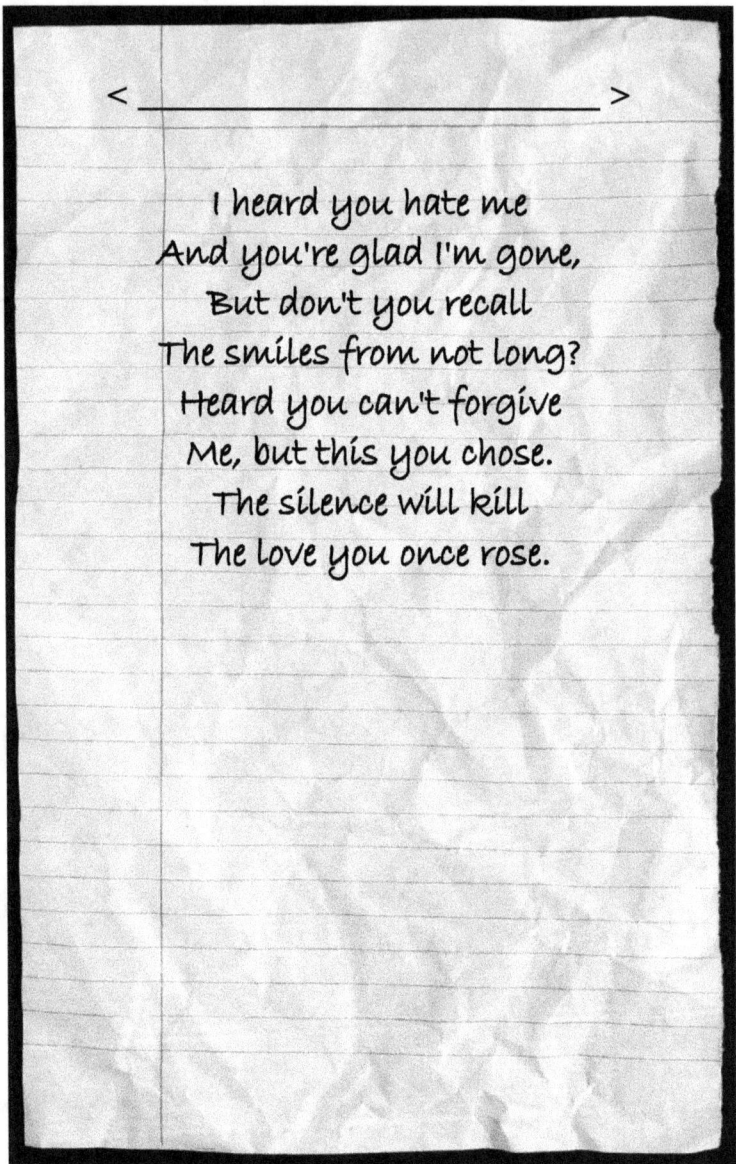

I heard you hate me
And you're glad I'm gone,
But don't you recall
The smiles from not long?
Heard you can't forgive
Me, but this you chose.
The silence will kill
The love you once rose.

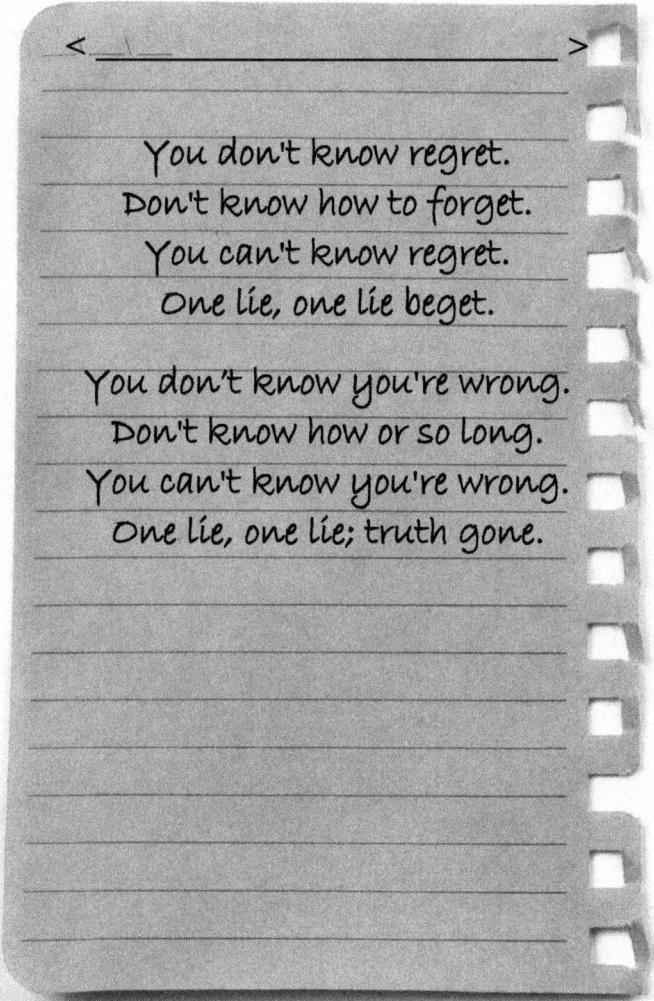

You don't know regret.
Don't know how to forget.
You can't know regret.
One lie, one lie beget.

You don't know you're wrong.
Don't know how or so long.
You can't know you're wrong.
One lie, one lie; truth gone.

< ——————————————— >

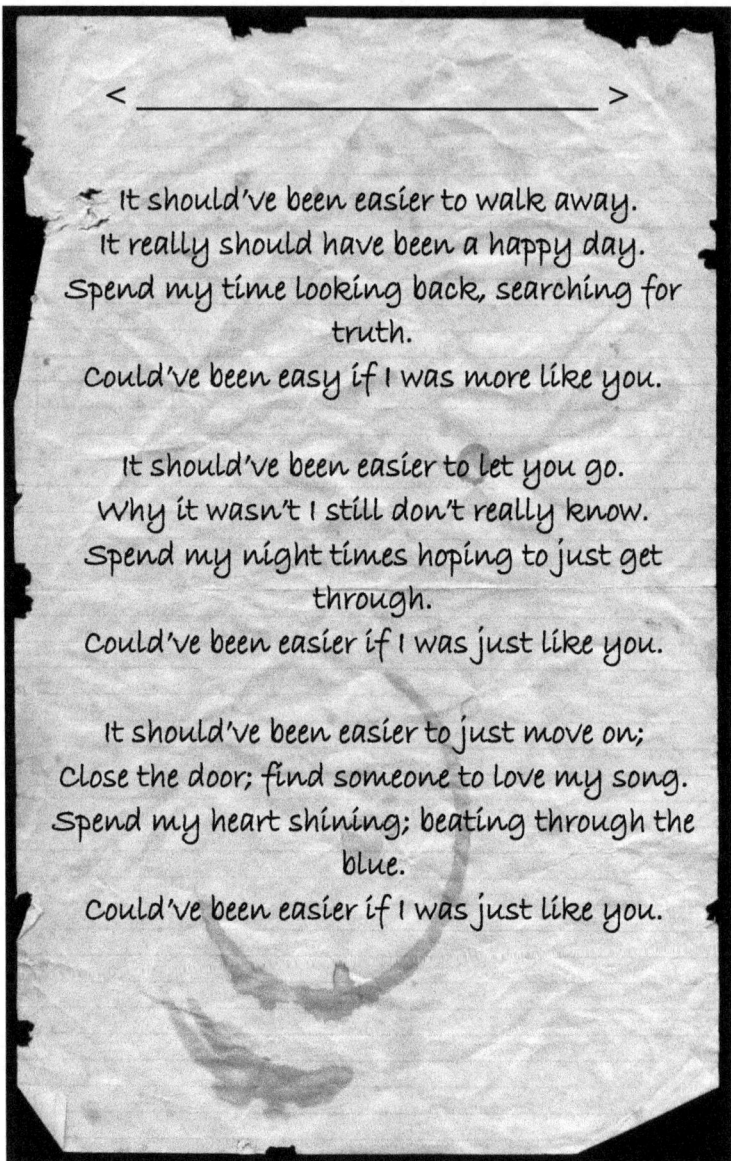

It should've been easier to walk away.
It really should have been a happy day.
Spend my time looking back, searching for
truth.
Could've been easy if I was more like you.

It should've been easier to let you go.
Why it wasn't I still don't really know.
Spend my night times hoping to just get
through.
Could've been easier if I was just like you.

It should've been easier to just move on;
Close the door; find someone to love my song.
Spend my heart shining; beating through the
blue.
Could've been easier if I was just like you.

< _____ >

My soul took a trip today:
Flew out toward the eagle's way;
Sailed across the ever high;
Saw my life from a brand new eye.

< _____ >

If I could breathe into the dead,
I could get over you.
If I could color the sky red,
I could get passed you.

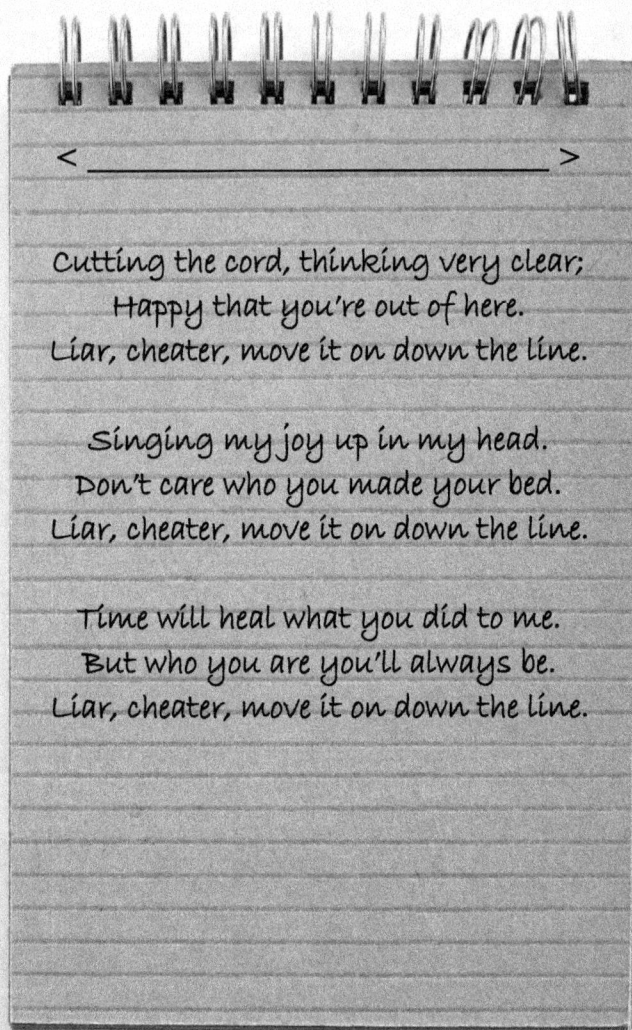

< ———————————————————— >

Cutting the cord, thinking very clear;
Happy that you're out of here.
Liar, cheater, move it on down the line.

Singing my joy up in my head.
Don't care who you made your bed.
Liar, cheater, move it on down the line.

Time will heal what you did to me.
But who you are you'll always be.
Liar, cheater, move it on down the line.

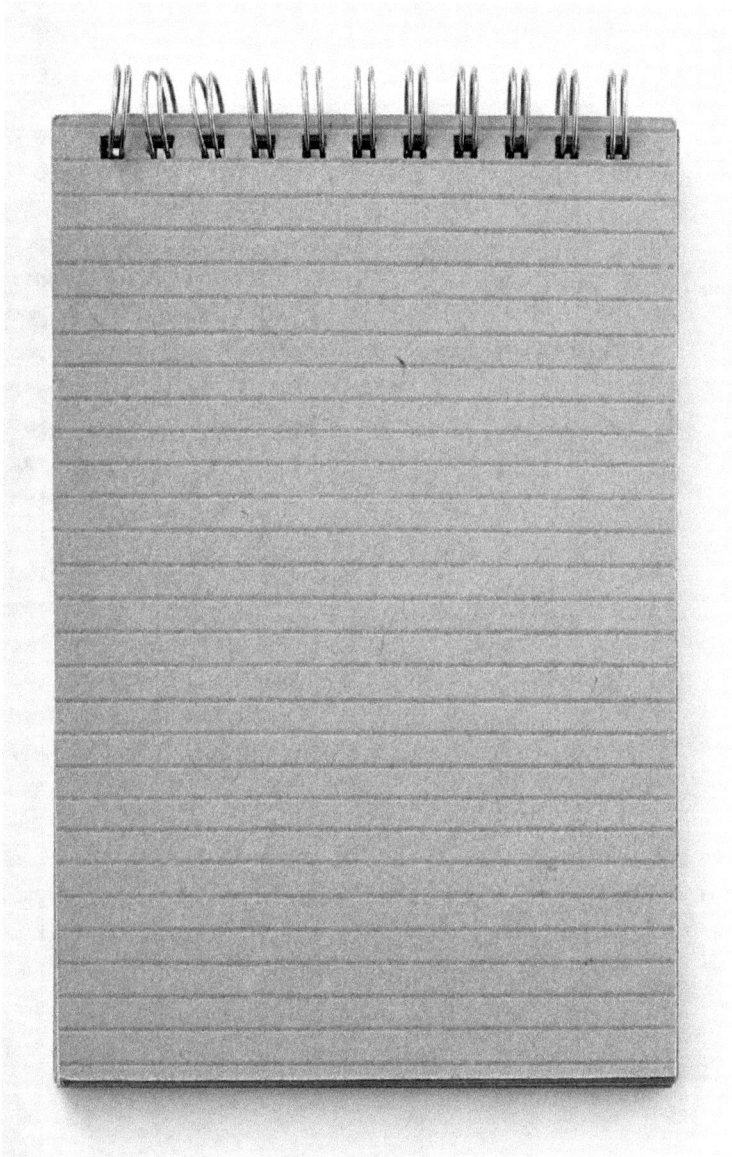

< _____ >

The lines on your map of time
Tell a story, yours and mine.
The fresh scars left by your wounds
Tell a horror, slashed and pruned.

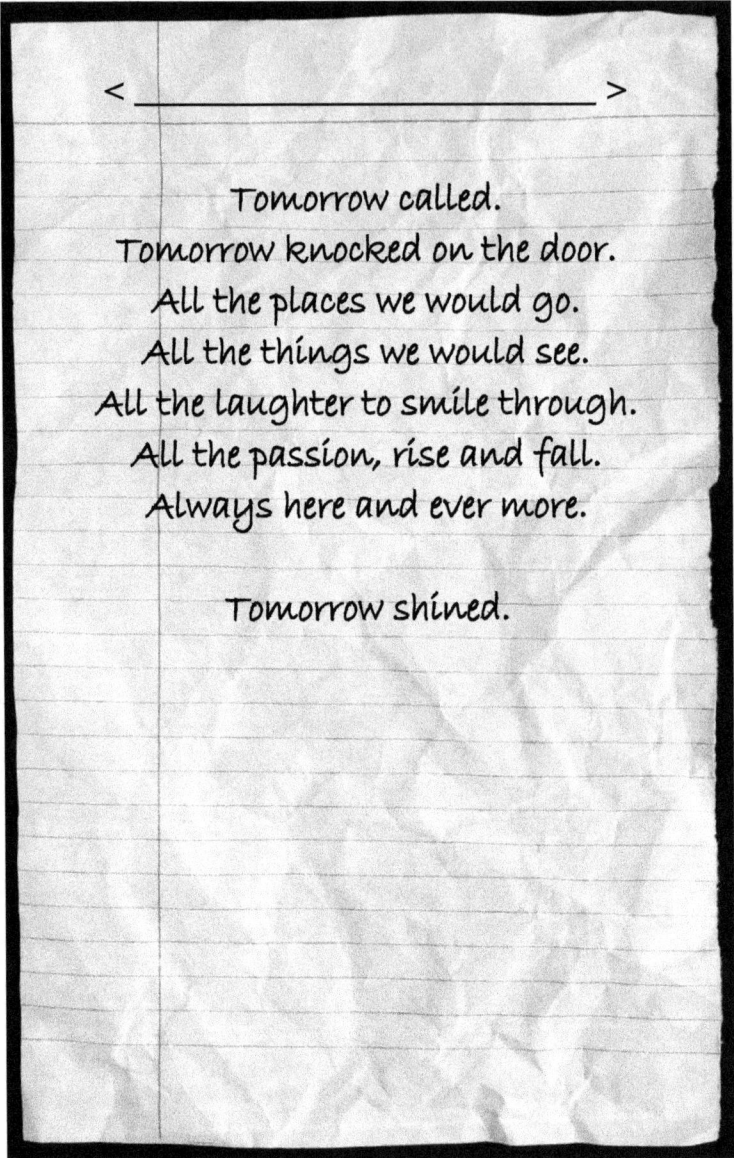

Tomorrow called.
Tomorrow knocked on the door.
All the places we would go.
All the things we would see.
All the laughter to smile through.
All the passion, rise and fall.
Always here and ever more.

Tomorrow shined.

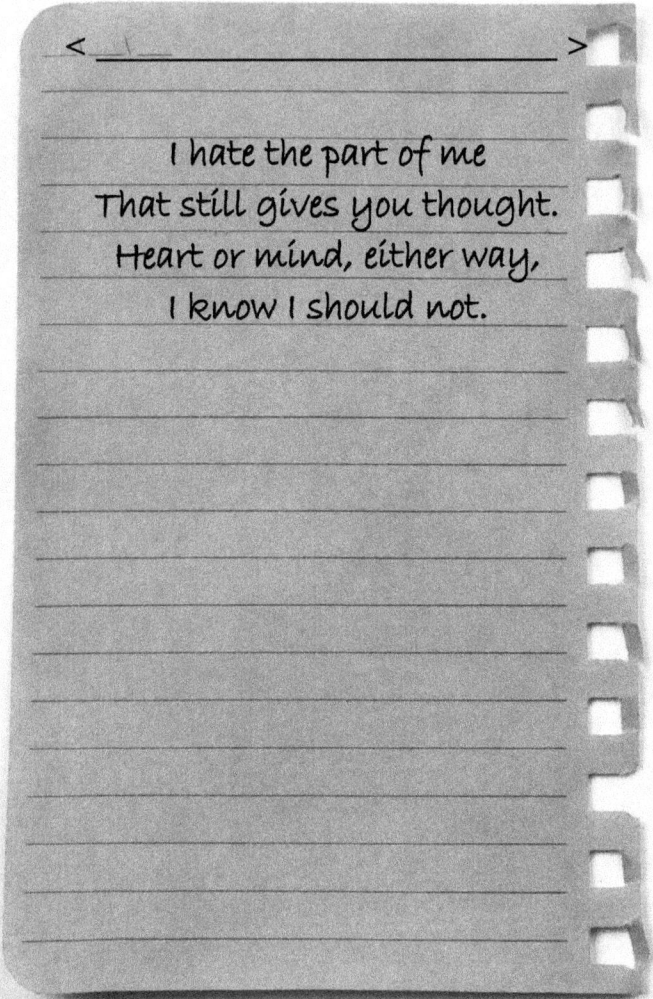

I hate the part of me
That still gives you thought.
Heart or mind, either way,
I know I should not.

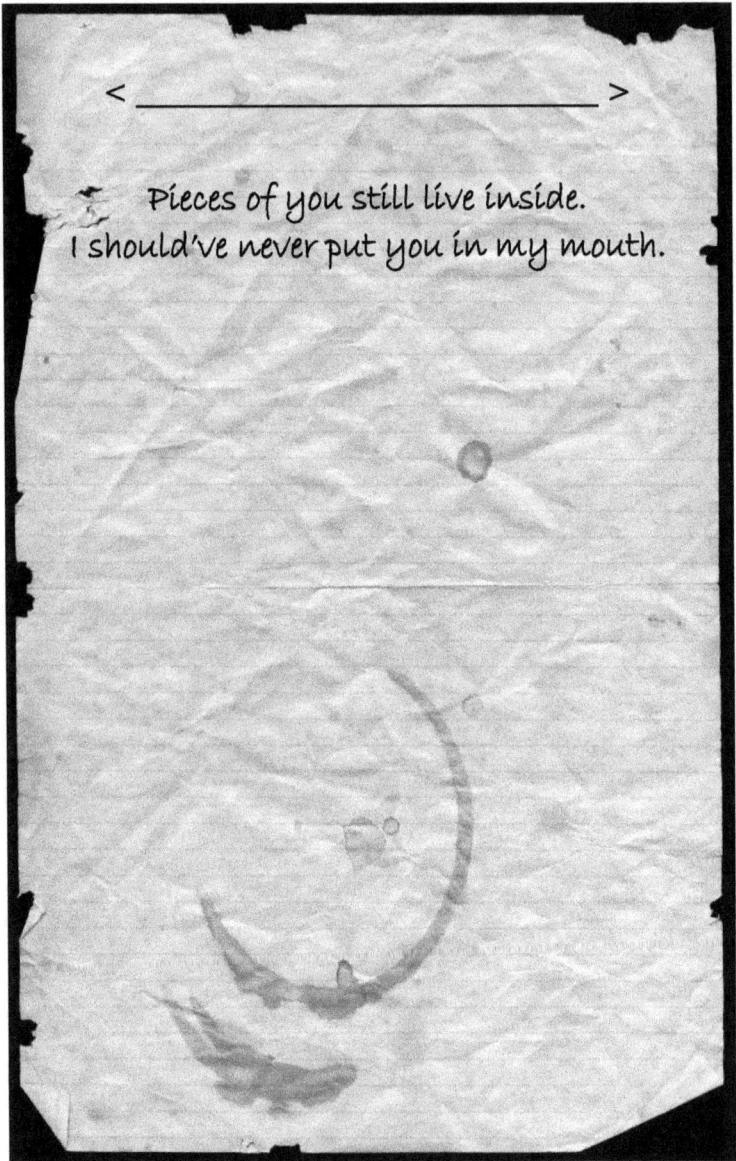

Pieces of you still live inside.
I should've never put you in my mouth.

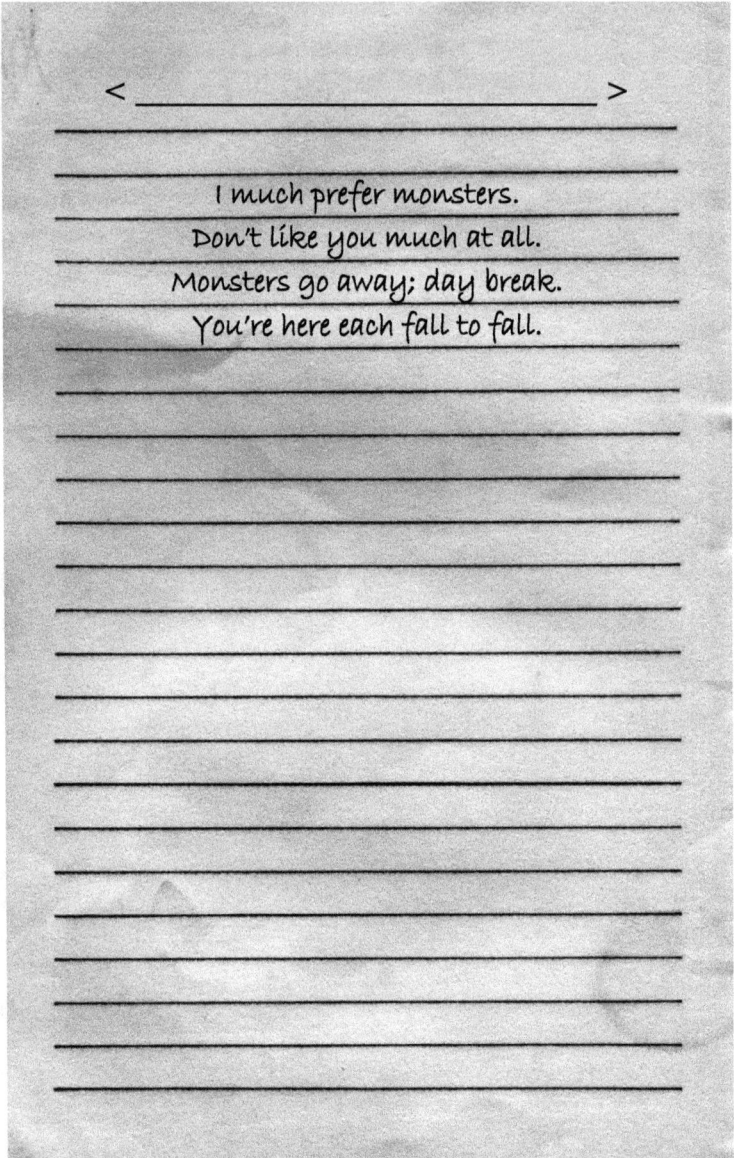

< _____ >

I much prefer monsters.
Don't like you much at all.
Monsters go away; day break.
You're here each fall to fall.

< _____ >

I heard your words
Through someone else's mouth,
Through someone else's voice.
Even still,
I could tell it was you.

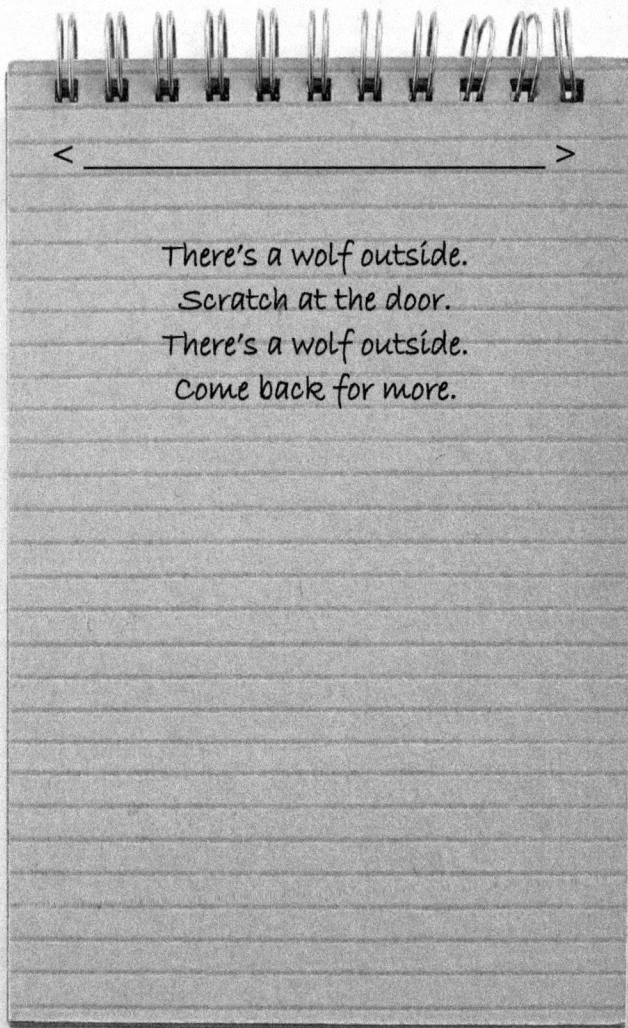

There's a wolf outside.
Scratch at the door.
There's a wolf outside.
Come back for more.

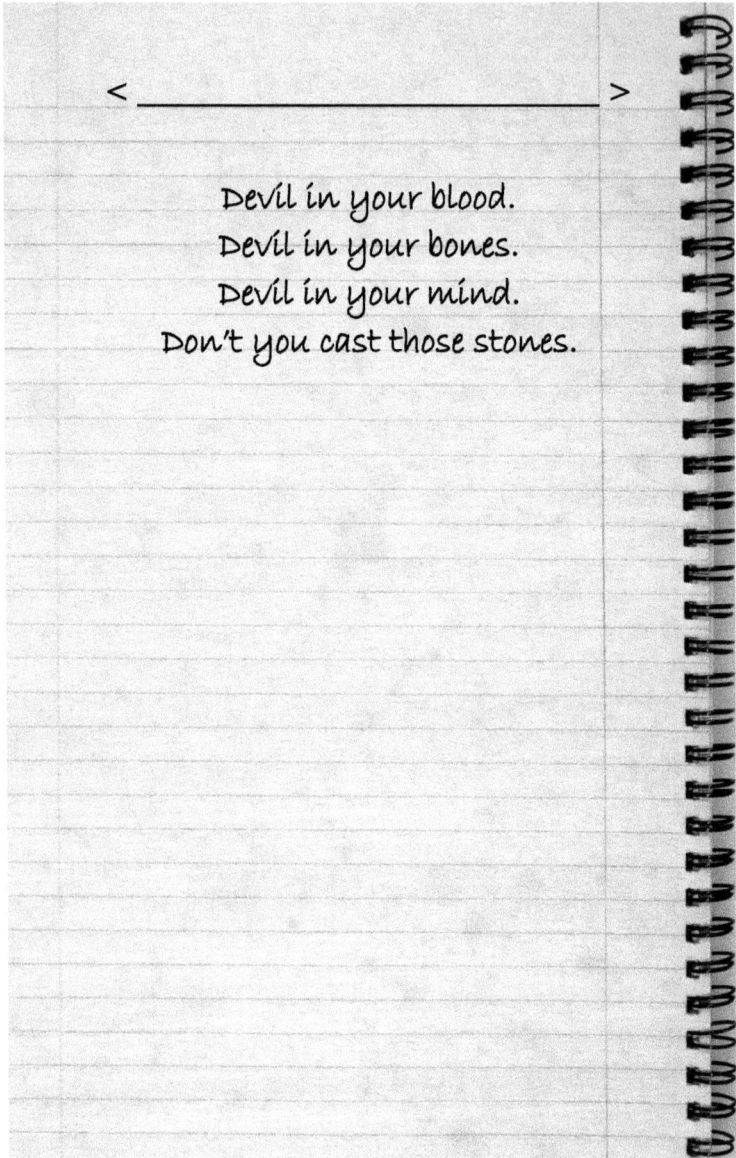

< _____ >

Devil in your blood.
Devil in your bones.
Devil in your mind.
Don't you cast those stones.

<   _____   >

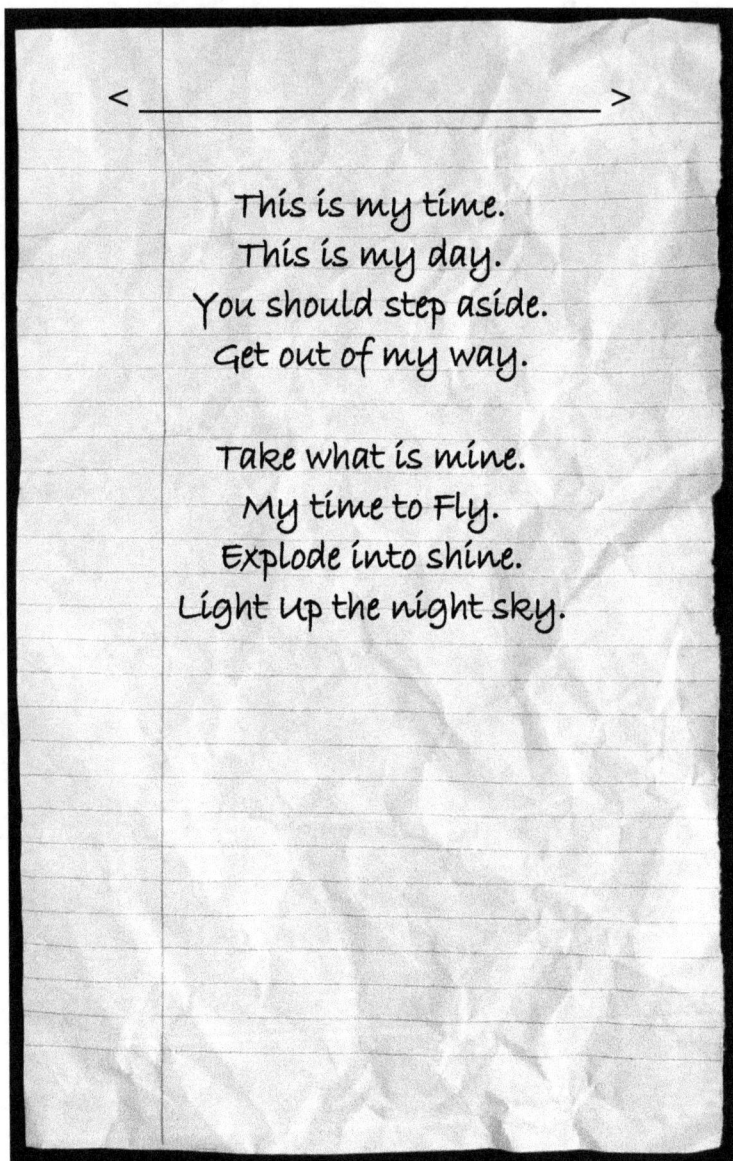

This is my time.
This is my day.
You should step aside.
Get out of my way.

Take what is mine.
My time to Fly.
Explode into shine.
Light Up the night sky.

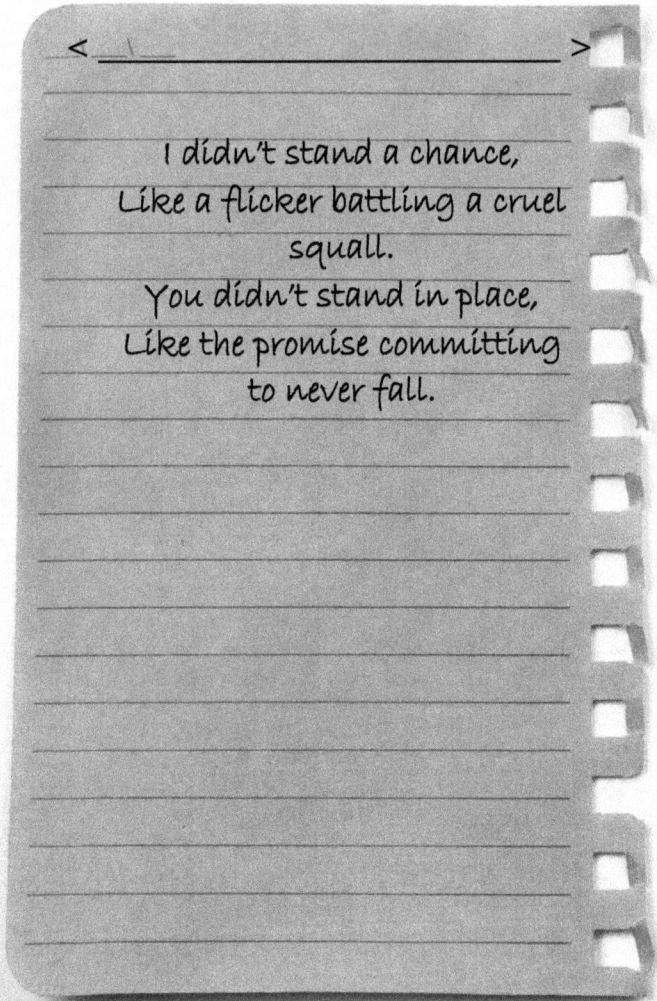

I didn't stand a chance,
Like a flicker battling a cruel
squall.
You didn't stand in place,
Like the promise committing
to never fall.

< ———————————————— >

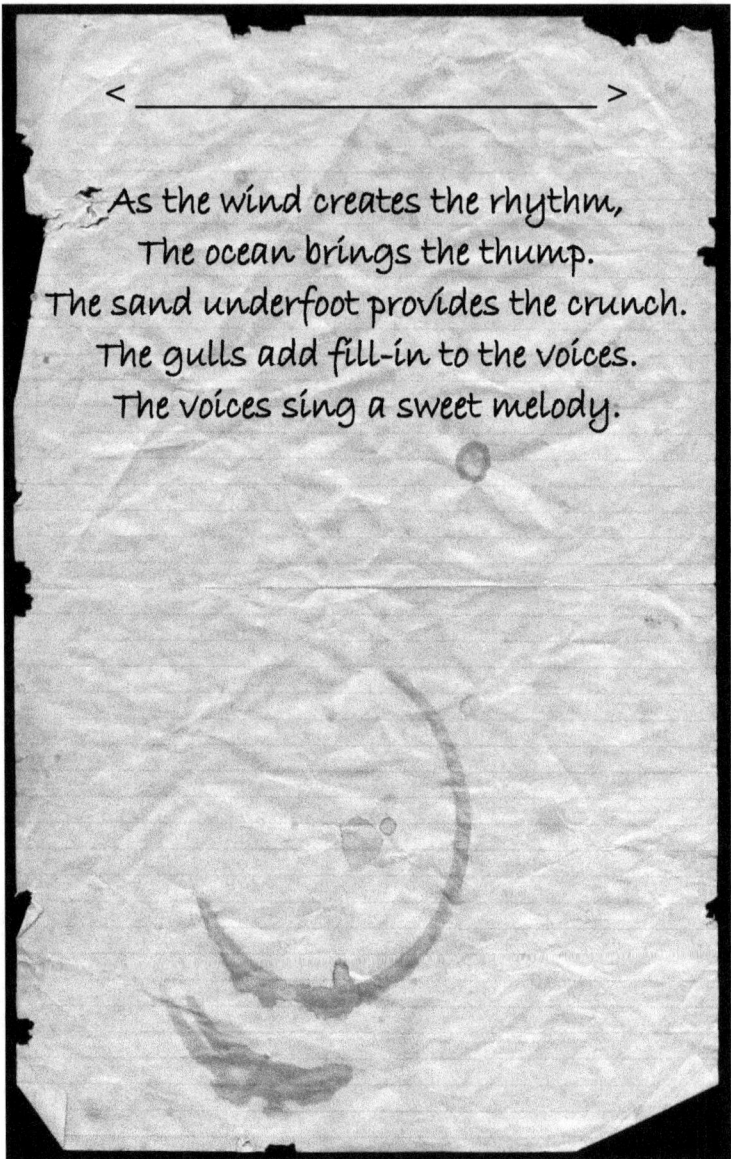

As the wind creates the rhythm,
The ocean brings the thump.
The sand underfoot provides the crunch.
The gulls add fill-in to the voices.
The voices sing a sweet melody.

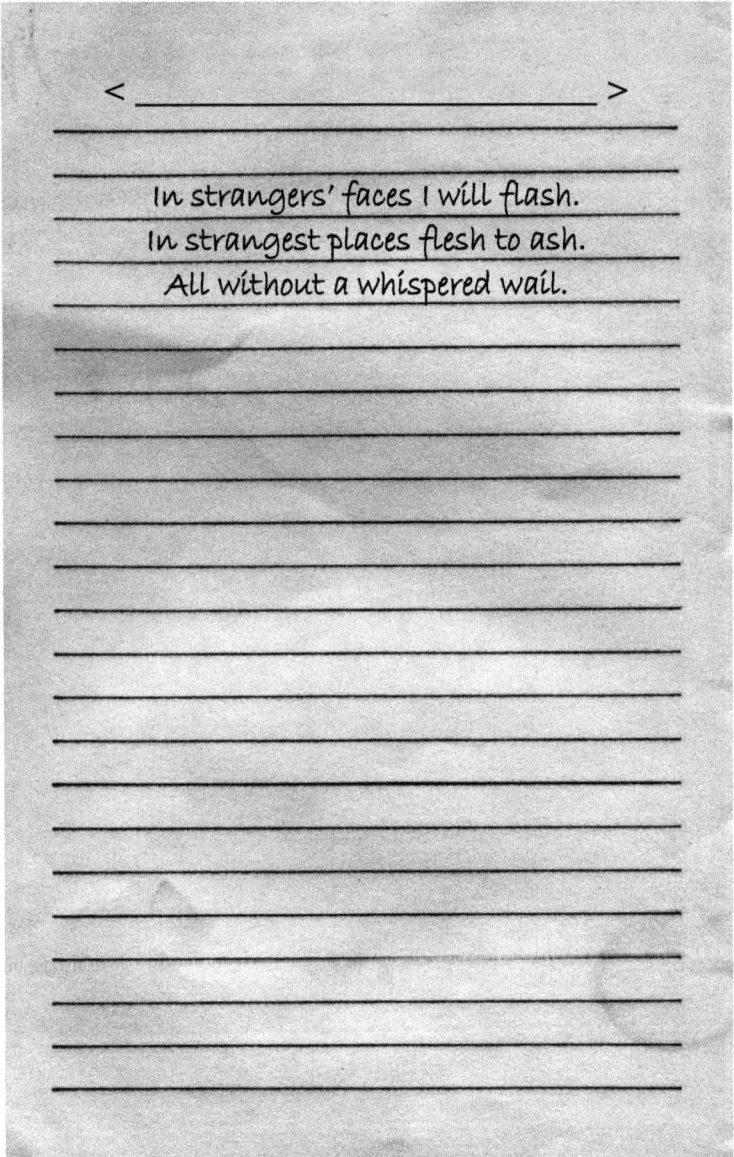

< _____ >

In strangers' faces I will flash.
In strangest places flesh to ash.
All without a whispered wail.

< ———————————————— >

How will you remember,
Remember my name;
Recall my laughter;
Evoke a memory;
Ponder my whereabouts;
Arouse a feeling;
Conjure an image;
Bethink a moment;
Reminisce a simple touch;
Recognize an utterance;
Relive a gentle kiss,
When I have swam the sands of time for a
thousand years?

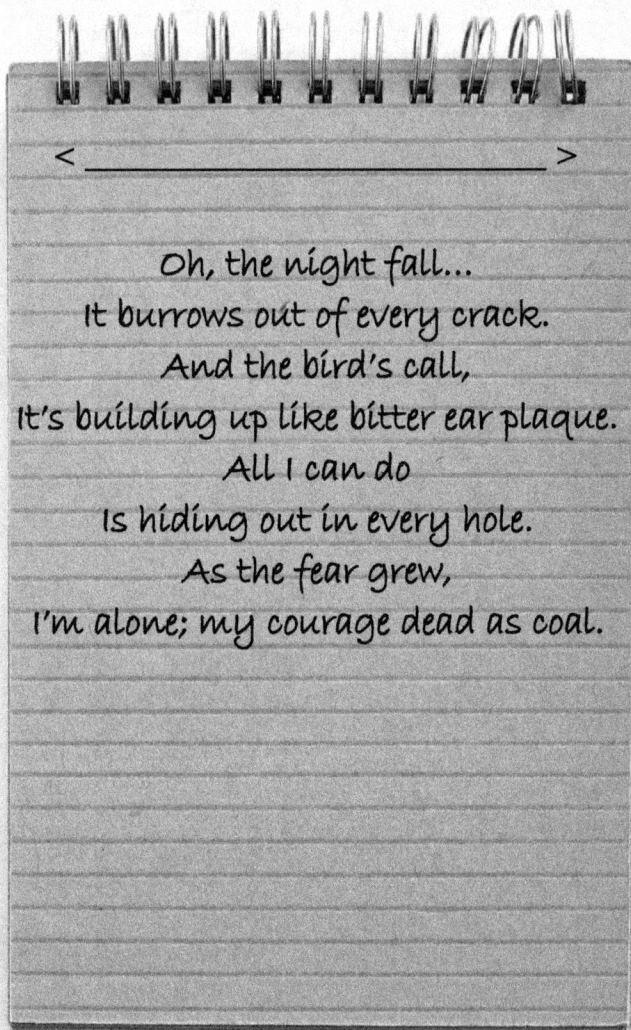

Oh, the night fall...
It burrows out of every crack.
And the bird's call,
It's building up like bitter ear plaque.
All I can do
Is hiding out in every hole.
As the fear grew,
I'm alone; my courage dead as coal.

I am returning
From between all space and time.
So much traveling,
Am covered in dirt and grime.
I am still healing
From rowing oceans dark, deep;
So far wandering
All meaning, away to creep.
Where am I going?
Where laying my head is done.
What does it matter?
All knowing will carry on.

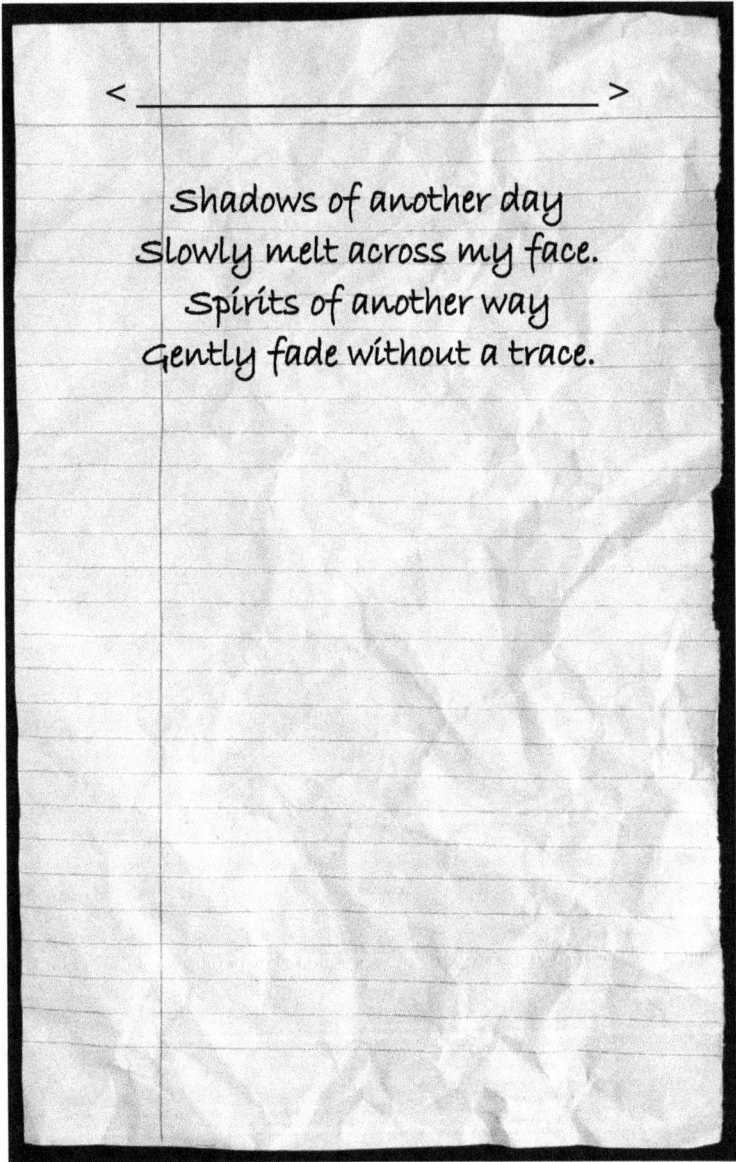

Shadows of another day
Slowly melt across my face.
Spirits of another way
Gently fade without a trace.

< _____ >

Today last year
Left a black spot on my soul
I've been looking for the White
out ever since I walked away.

Today this year
Look at me, still tall and
strong.
I've been building a new four
walled world out of pieces left
behind.

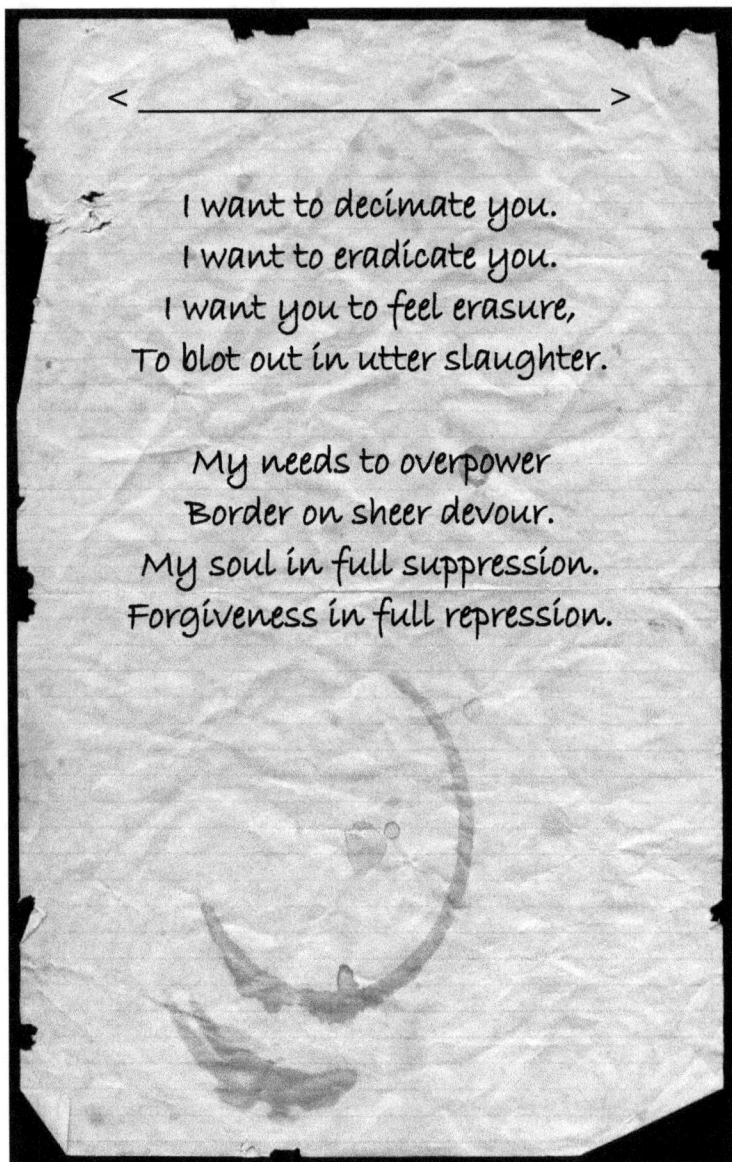

I want to decimate you.
I want to eradicate you.
I want you to feel erasure,
To blot out in utter slaughter.

My needs to overpower
Border on sheer devour.
My soul in full suppression.
Forgiveness in full repression.

< _____ >

Silver gray clouds stream against the pitch black sky.

Traveling to nowhere on this moonless night.

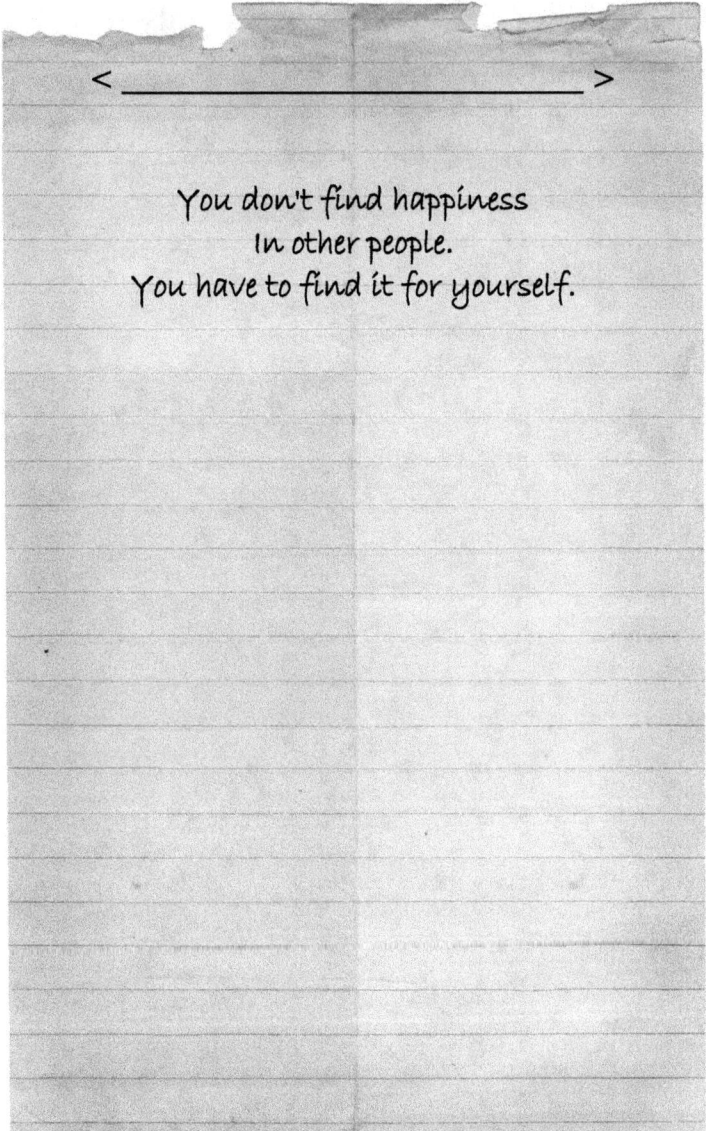

You don't find happiness
In other people.
You have to find it for yourself.

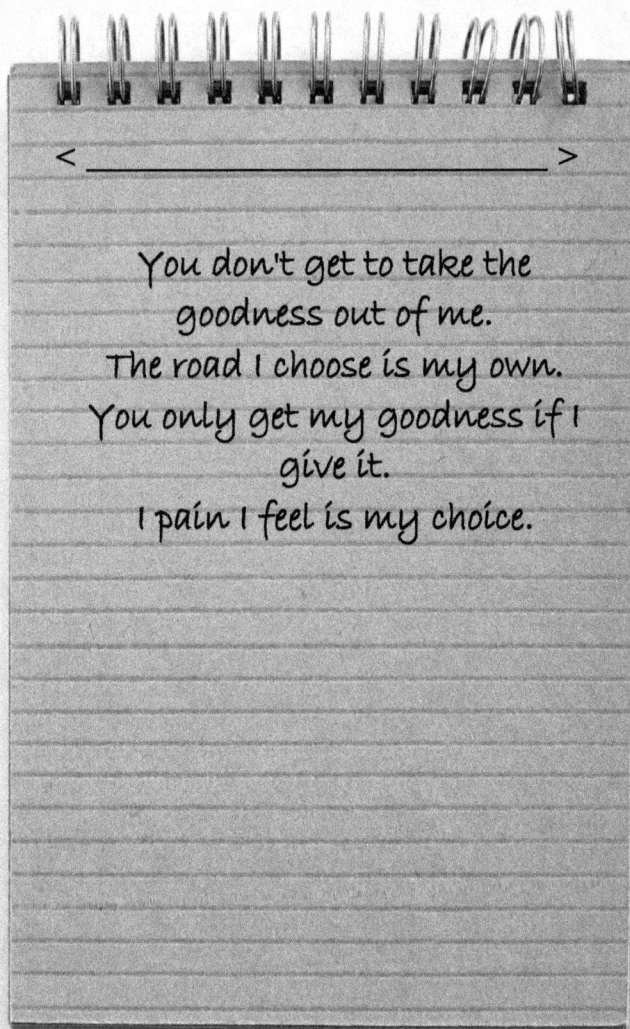

You don't get to take the
goodness out of me.
The road I choose is my own.
You only get my goodness if I
give it.
I pain I feel is my choice.

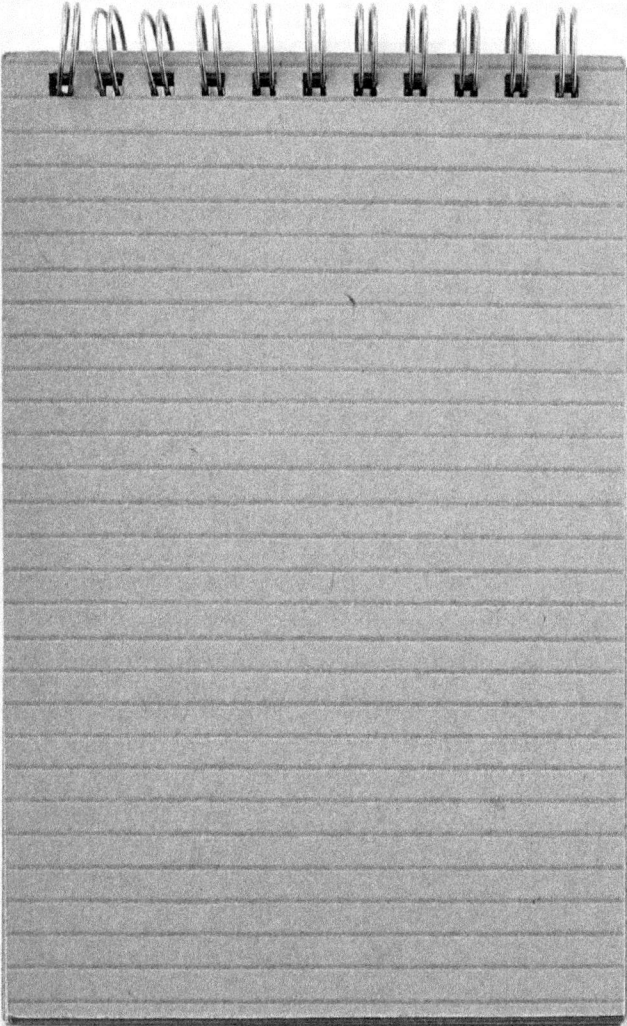

< _____ >

2 – So glad.

4 – So glad for now.

6 – So glad I feel brand new.

8 – So glad I got out in one piece.

10 – So glad today is here and I am me.

12 – So glad yesterday is over and you are you.

14 – So glad to hold tomorrow's hand while searching for bright skies.

16 – So glad your betrayal's pain taught me more about being human.

18 – So glad I don't have to walk around hiding my sins from all those I know.

20 – So glad for the future's promise; it's beckoning call, and for smiles that don't hide lies

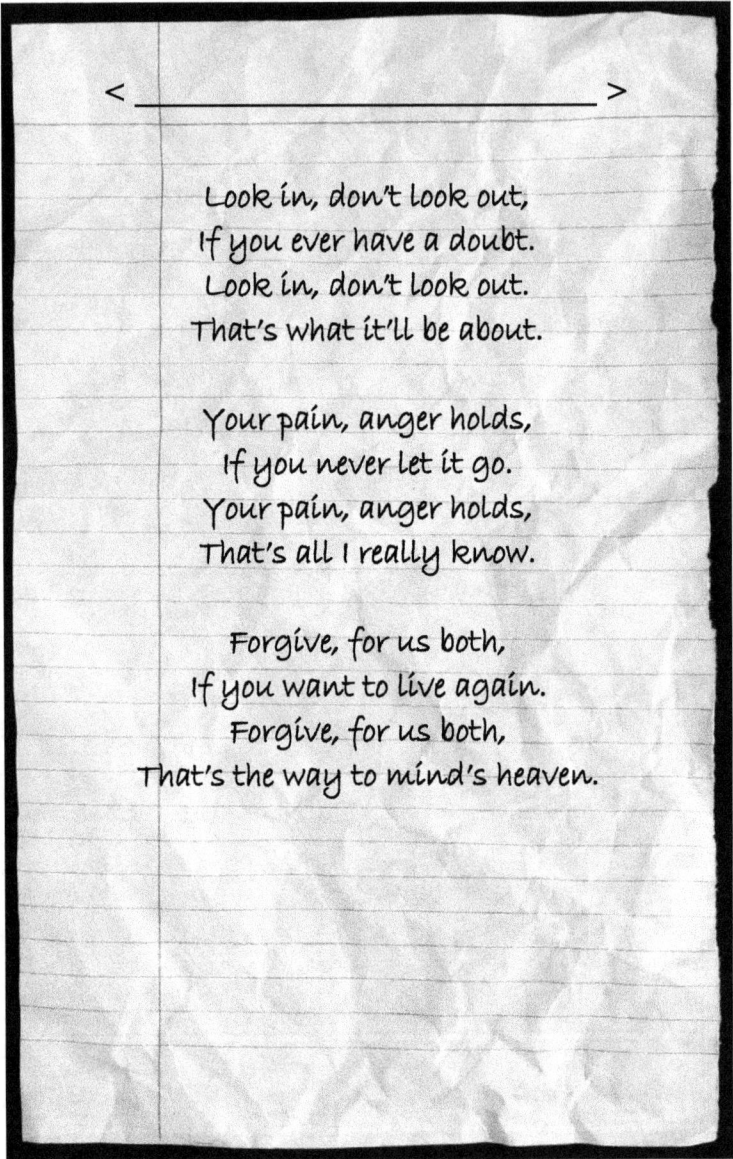

Look in, don't look out,
If you ever have a doubt.
Look in, don't look out.
That's what it'll be about.

Your pain, anger holds,
If you never let it go.
Your pain, anger holds,
That's all I really know.

Forgive, for us both,
If you want to live again.
Forgive, for us both,
That's the way to mind's heaven.

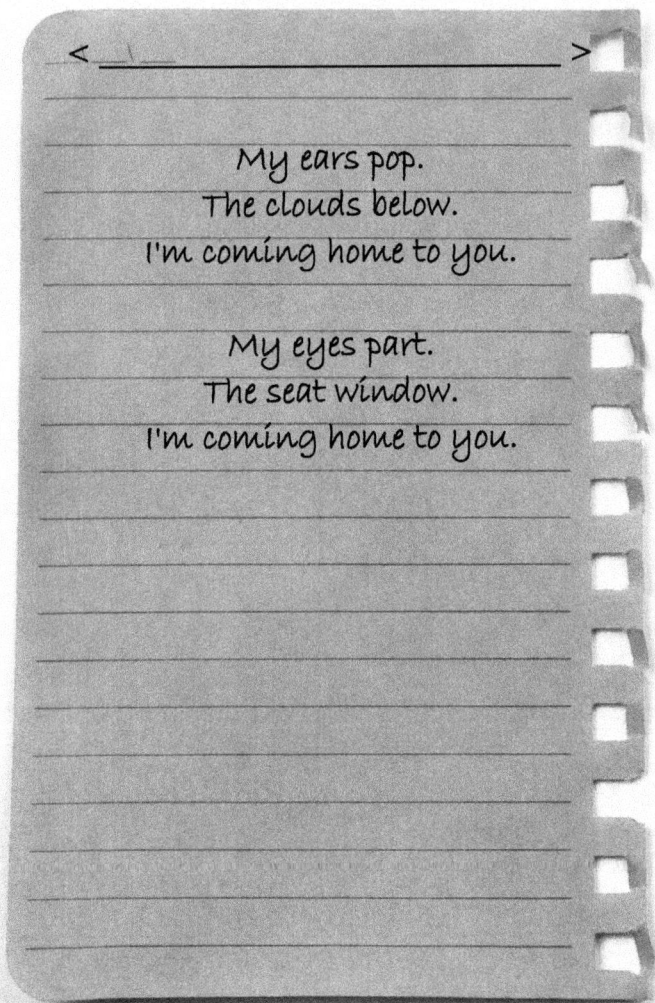

My ears pop.
The clouds below.
I'm coming home to you.

My eyes part.
The seat window.
I'm coming home to you.

< ──────────────────── >

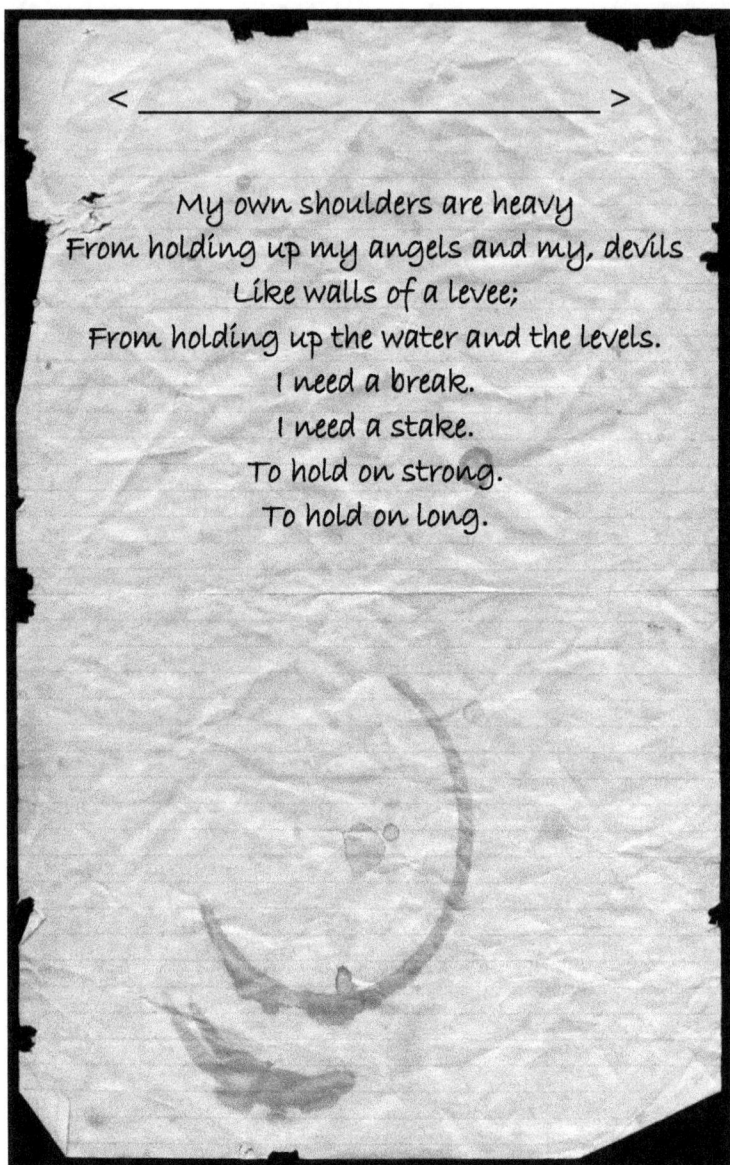

My own shoulders are heavy
From holding up my angels and my, devils
Like walls of a levee;
From holding up the water and the levels.
I need a break.
I need a stake.
To hold on strong.
To hold on long.

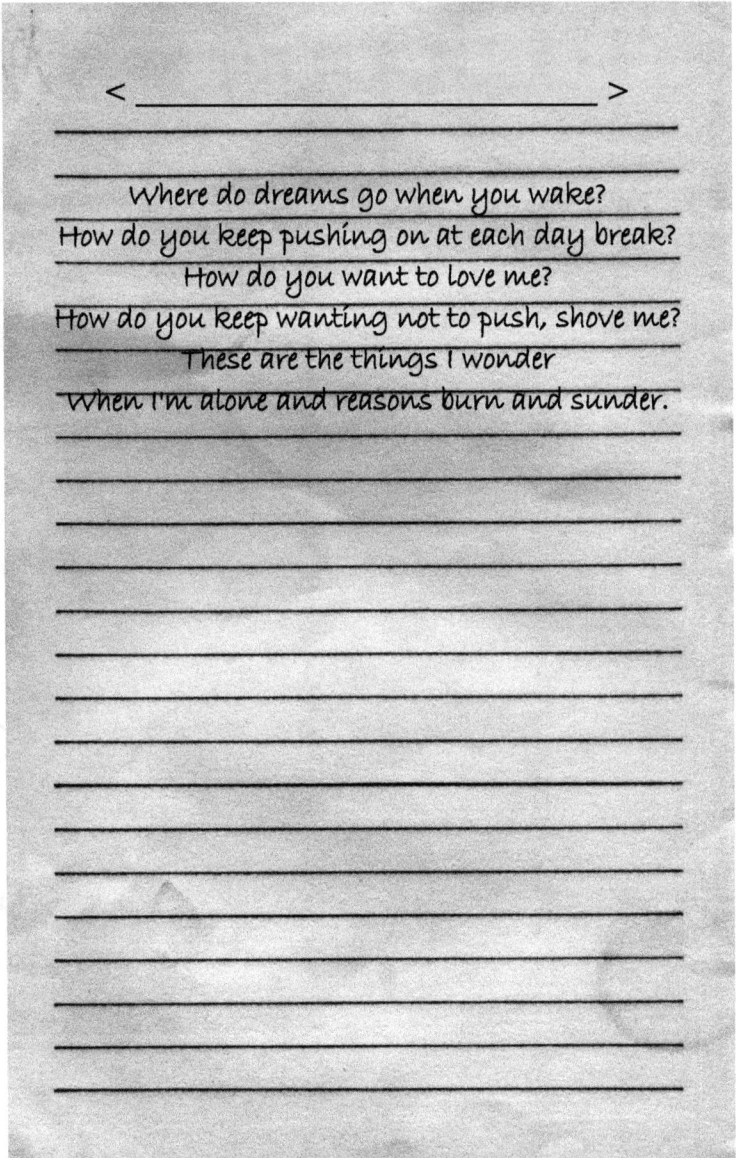

< _____ >

Where do dreams go when you wake?
How do you keep pushing on at each day break?
How do you want to love me?
How do you keep wanting not to push, shove me?
These are the things I wonder
When I'm alone and reasons burn and sunder.

Lead me to the sunshine
And push away a gray cloud.
Show me where lovers pine
And songs bellow out so loud.

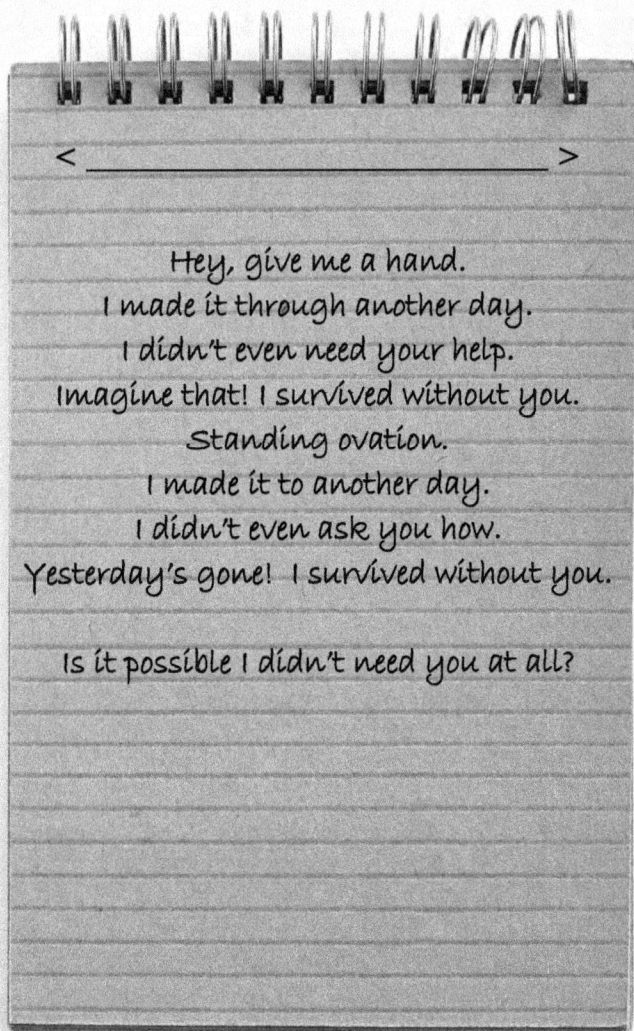

Hey, give me a hand.
I made it through another day.
I didn't even need your help.
Imagine that! I survived without you.
Standing ovation.
I made it to another day.
I didn't even ask you how.
Yesterday's gone! I survived without you.

Is it possible I didn't need you at all?

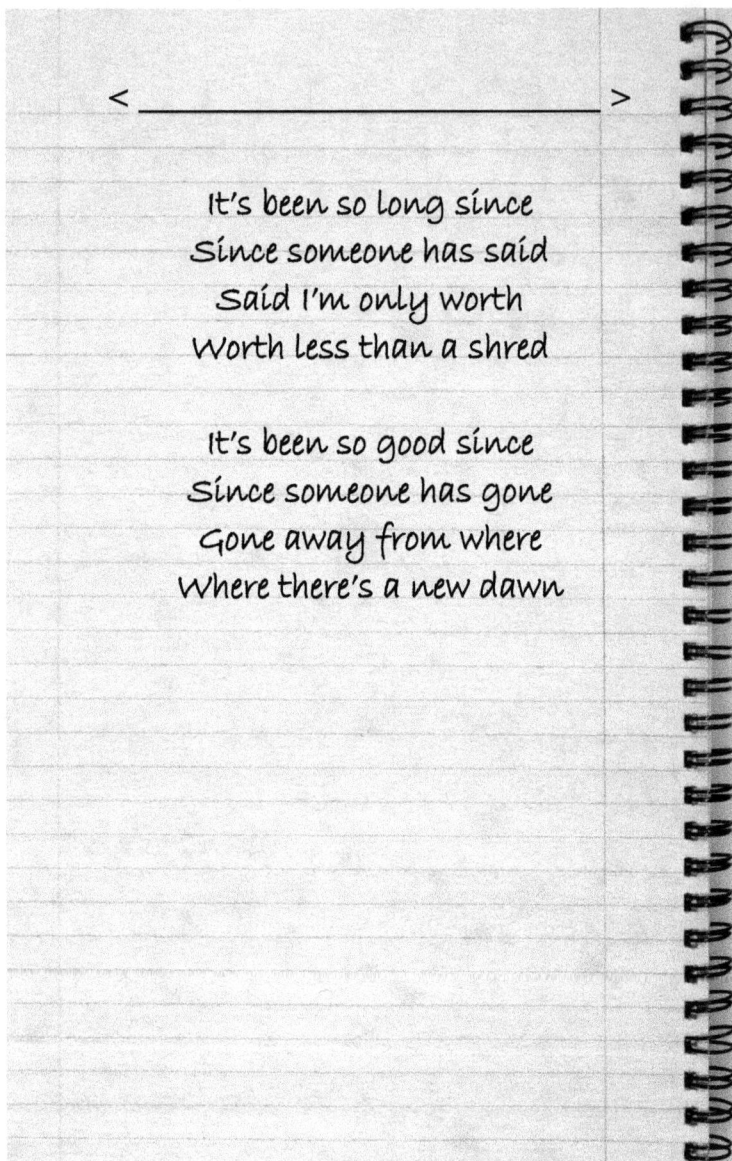

It's been so long since
Since someone has said
Said I'm only worth
Worth less than a shred

It's been so good since
Since someone has gone
Gone away from where
Where there's a new dawn

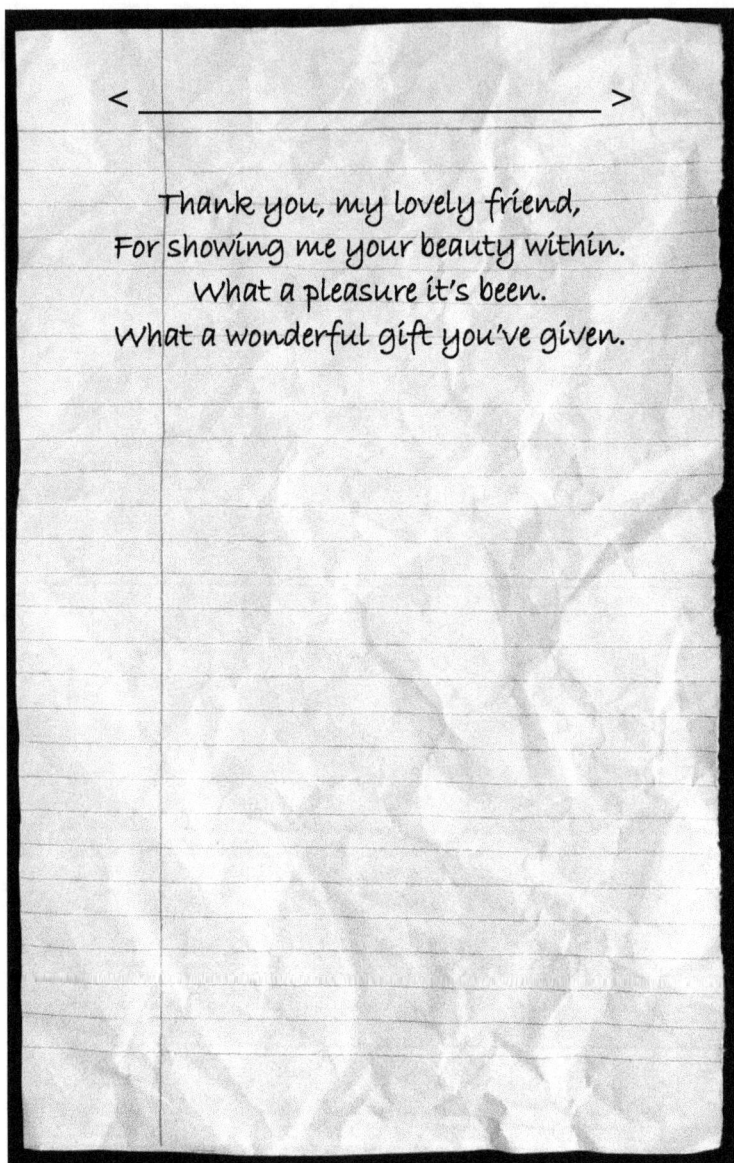

< _____ >

Thank you, my lovely friend,
For showing me your beauty within.
What a pleasure it's been.
What a wonderful gift you've given.

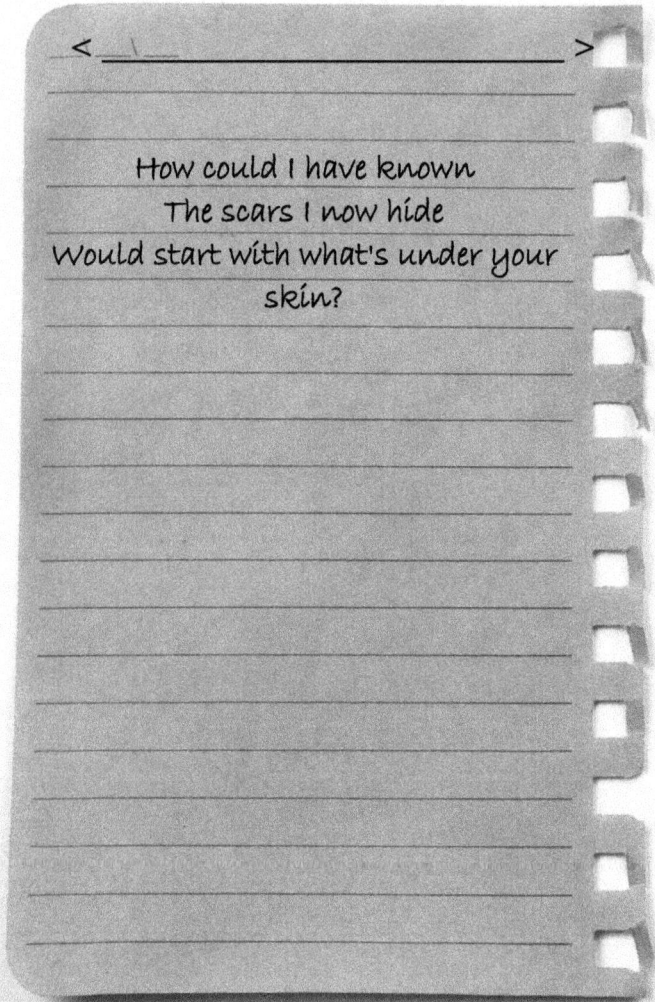

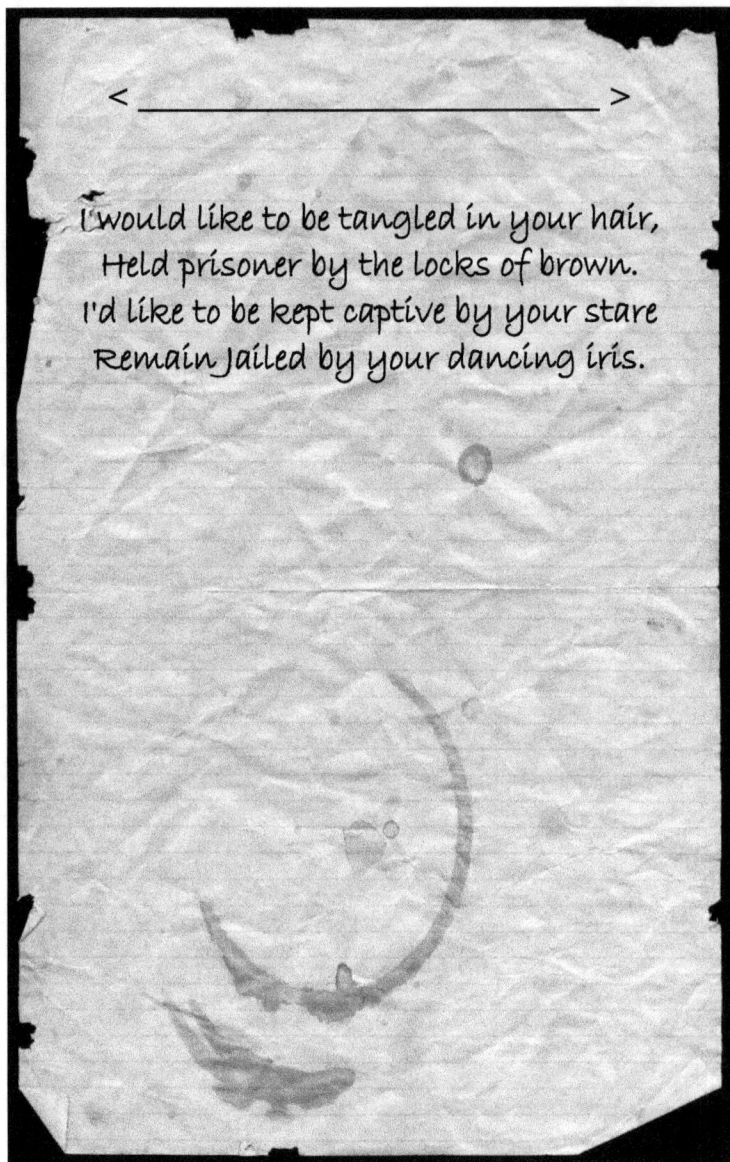

I would like to be tangled in your hair,
Held prisoner by the locks of brown.
I'd like to be kept captive by your stare
Remain jailed by your dancing iris.

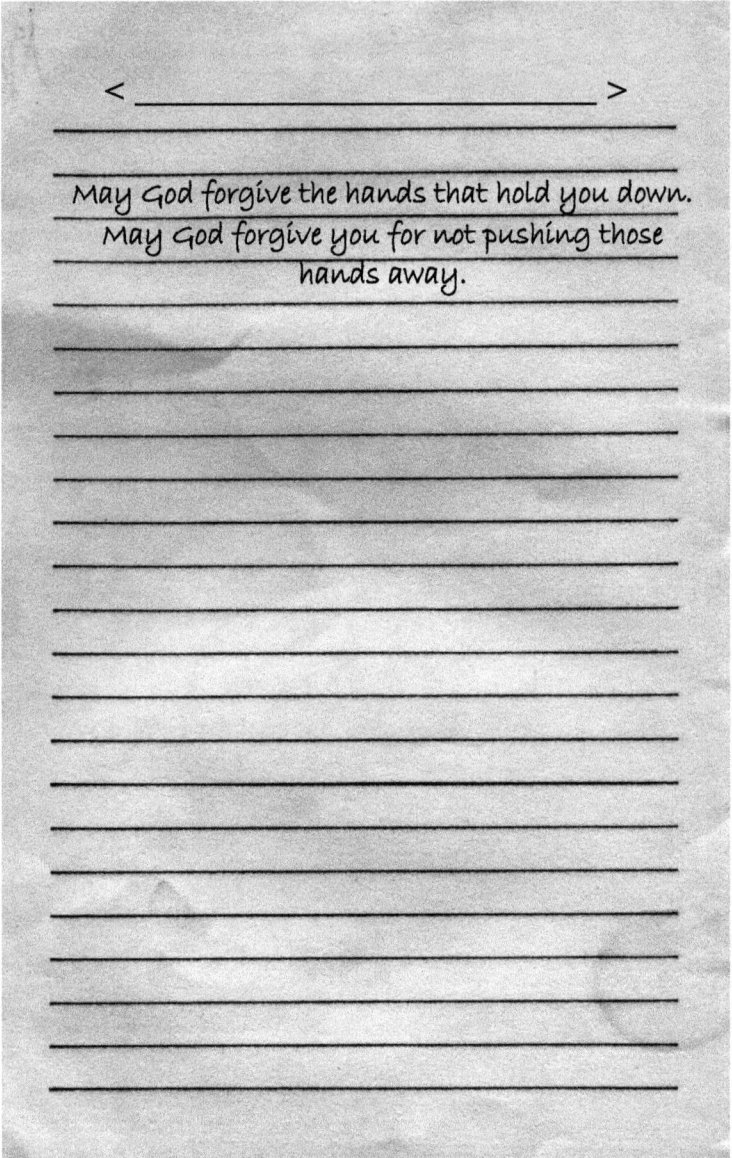

May God forgive the hands that hold you down. May God forgive you for not pushing those hands away.

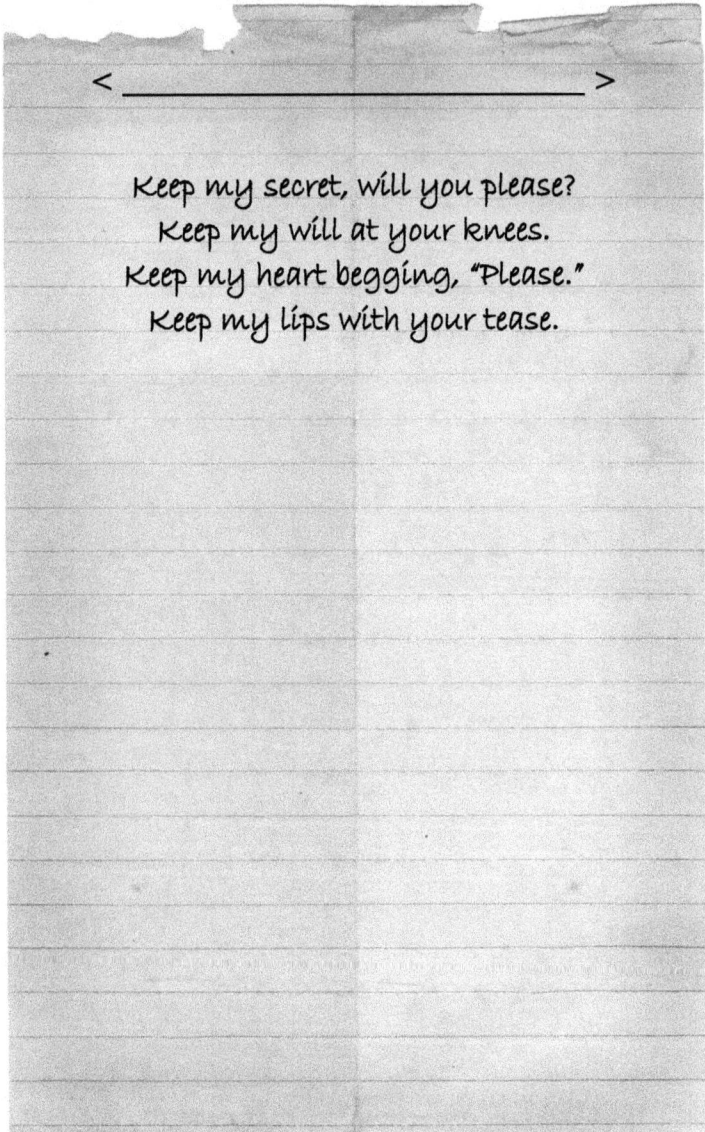

Keep my secret, will you please?
Keep my will at your knees.
Keep my heart begging, "Please."
Keep my lips with your tease.

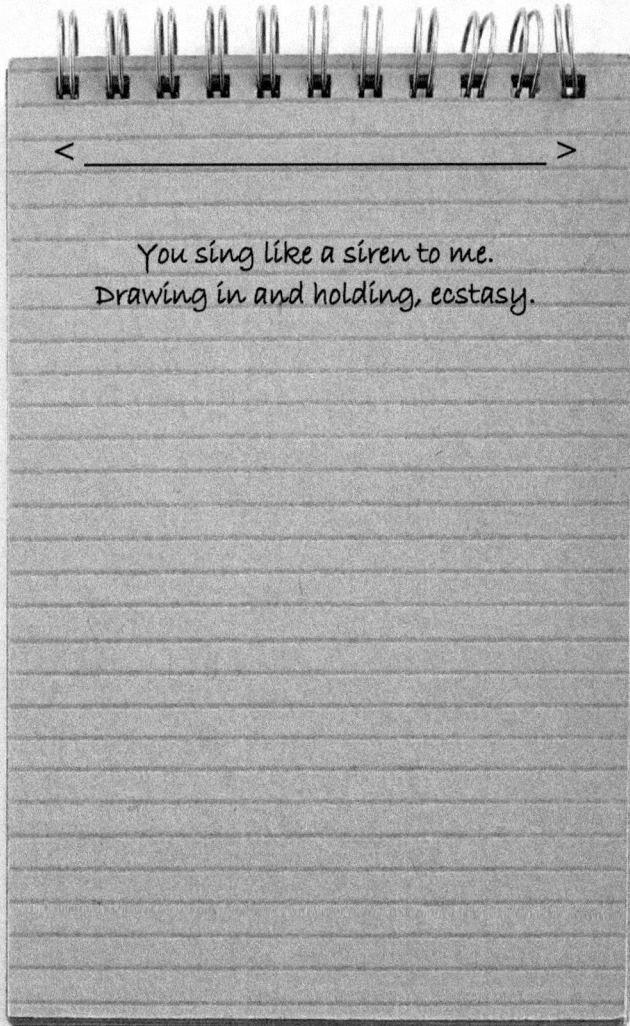

You sing like a siren to me.
Drawing in and holding, ecstasy.

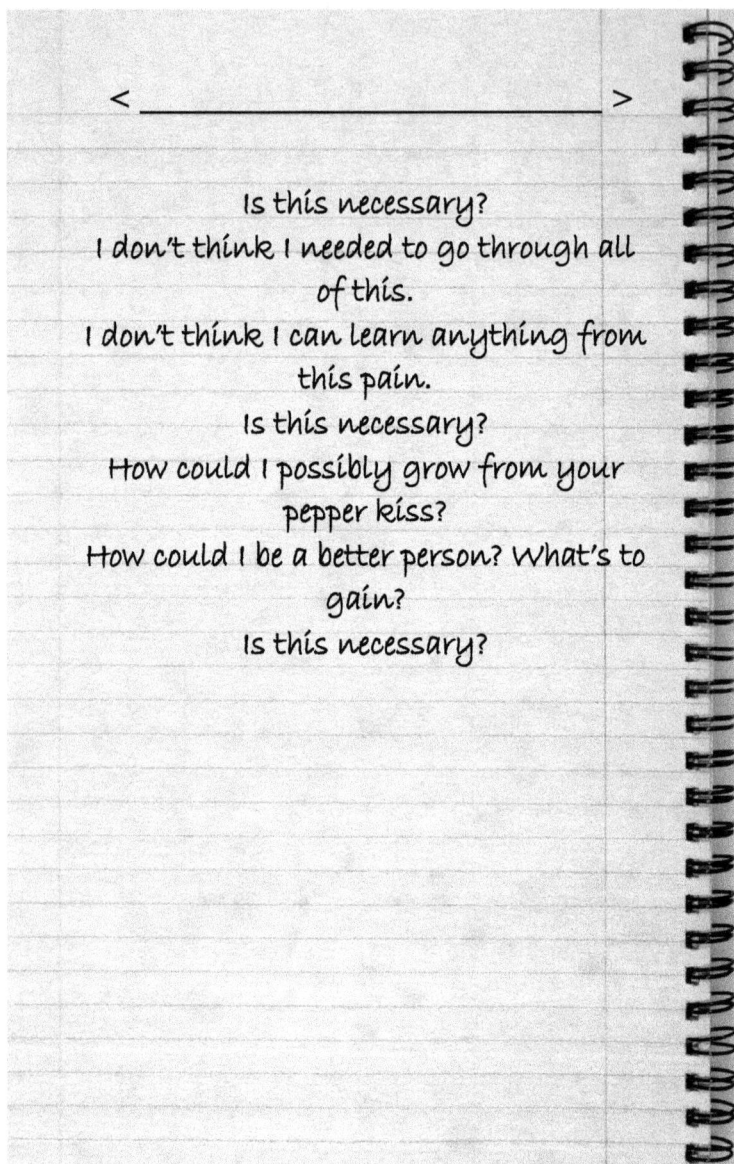

< _____ >

Is this necessary?
I don't think I needed to go through all
of this.
I don't think I can learn anything from
this pain.
Is this necessary?
How could I possibly grow from your
pepper kiss?
How could I be a better person? What's to
gain?
Is this necessary?

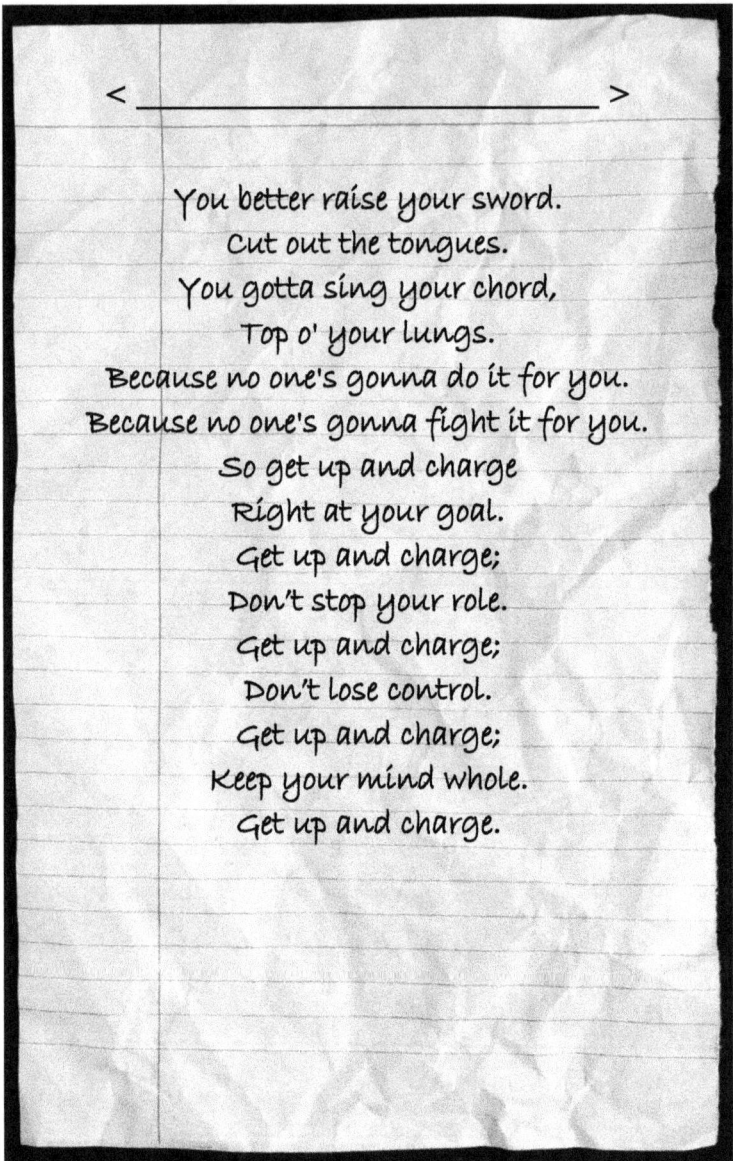

< _____ >

You better raise your sword.
Cut out the tongues.
You gotta sing your chord,
Top o' your lungs.
Because no one's gonna do it for you.
Because no one's gonna fight it for you.
So get up and charge
Right at your goal.
Get up and charge;
Don't stop your role.
Get up and charge;
Don't lose control.
Get up and charge;
Keep your mind whole.
Get up and charge.

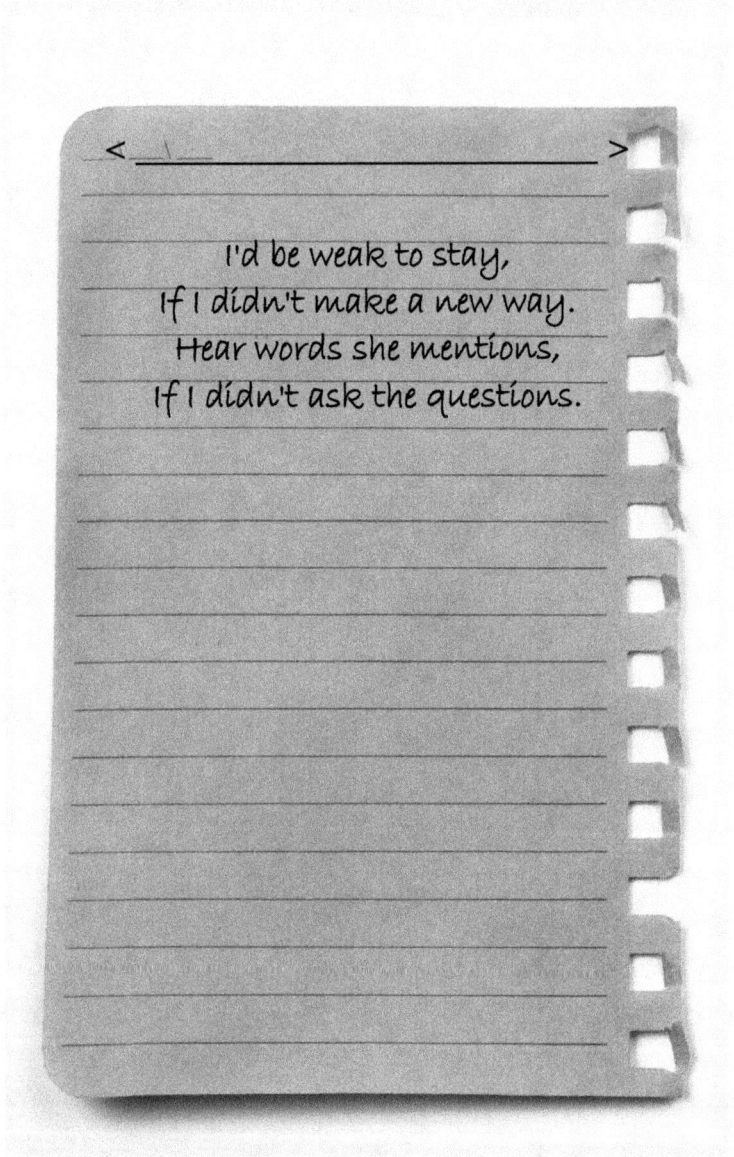

I'd be weak to stay,
If I didn't make a new way.
Hear words she mentions,
If I didn't ask the questions.

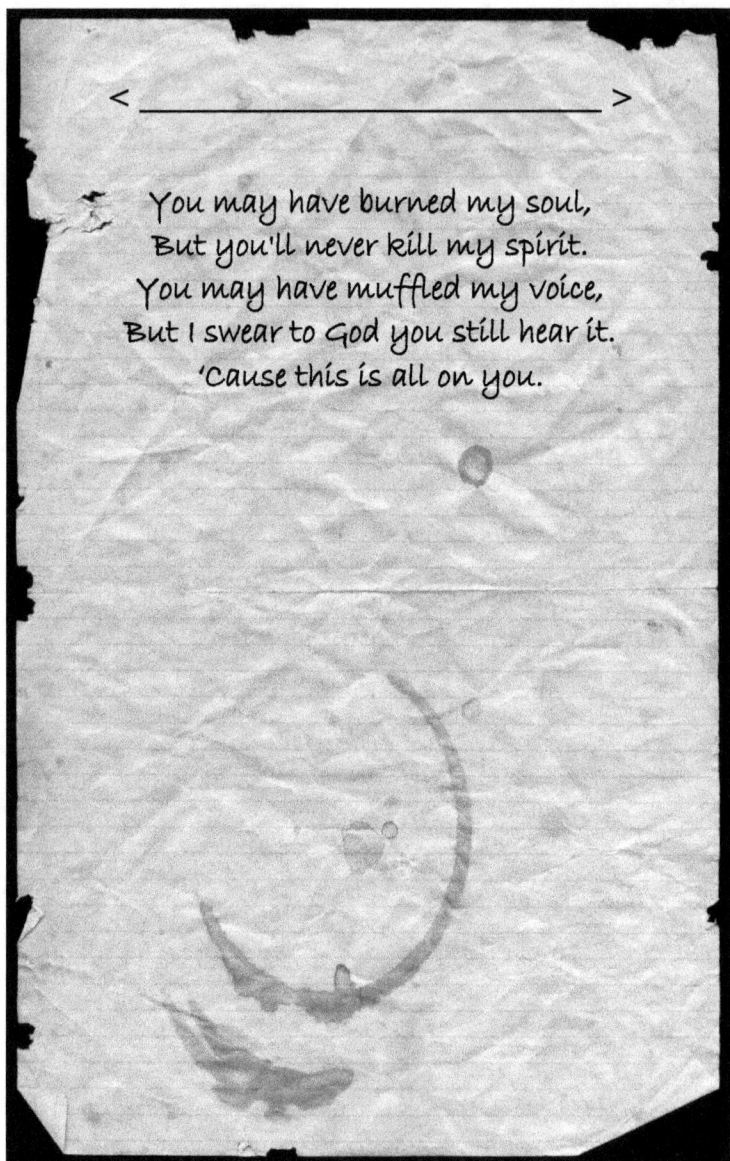

You may have burned my soul,
But you'll never kill my spirit.
You may have muffled my voice,
But I swear to God you still hear it.
'Cause this is all on you.

< _____ >

My moral compass is free of magnetic distractions.
How's yours?
My spirit _____ is free of

How's yours?

< _____ >

Your smile carries me step by step.
Funny how a so little means so much.
Your song settles me word by word.
Funny how the sweet refrains, like hands,
clutch.

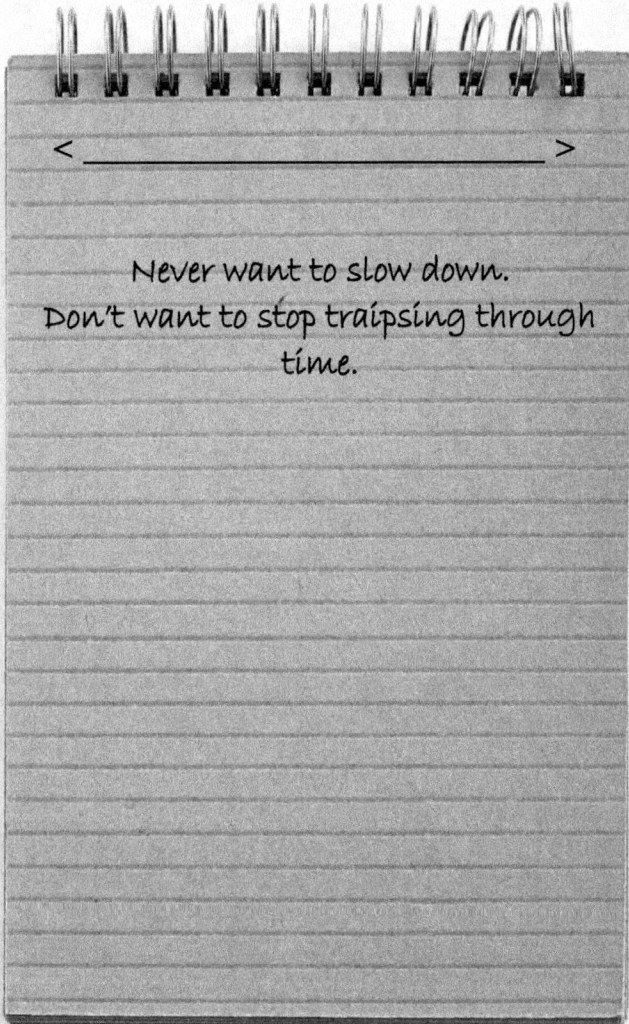

Never want to slow down.
Don't want to stop traipsing through time.

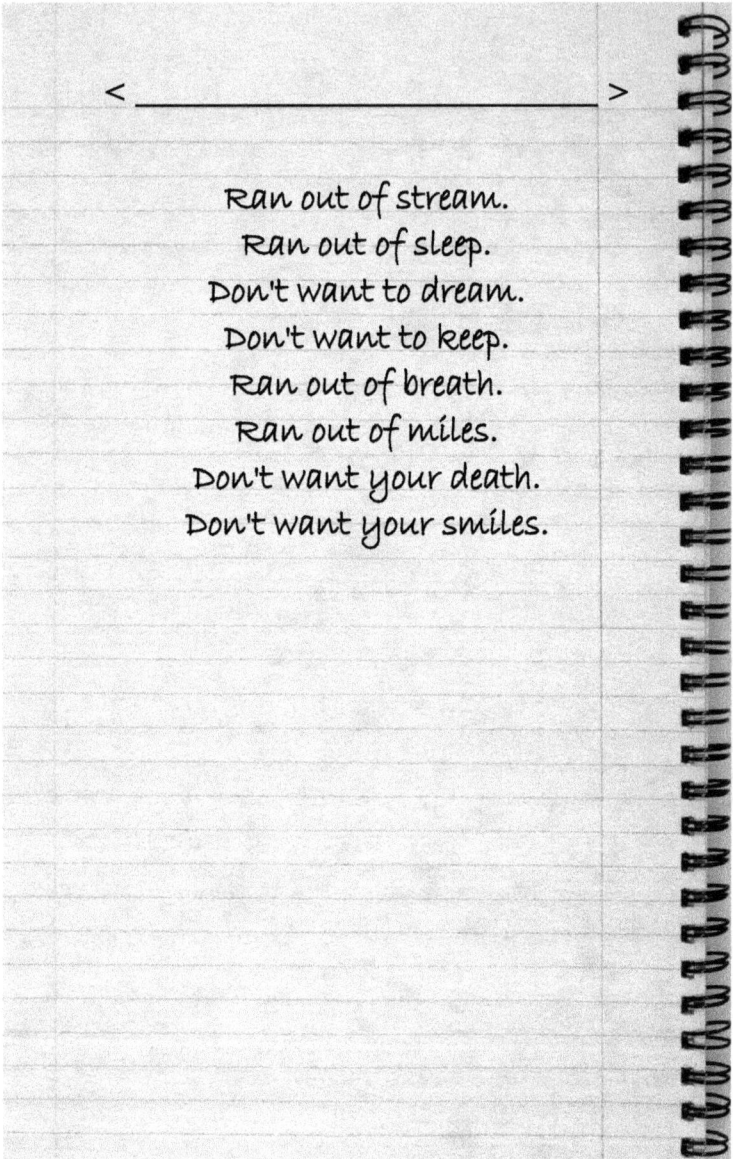

<

_____

>

Ran out of stream.
Ran out of sleep.
Don't want to dream.
Don't want to keep.
Ran out of breath.
Ran out of miles.
Don't want your death.
Don't want your smiles.

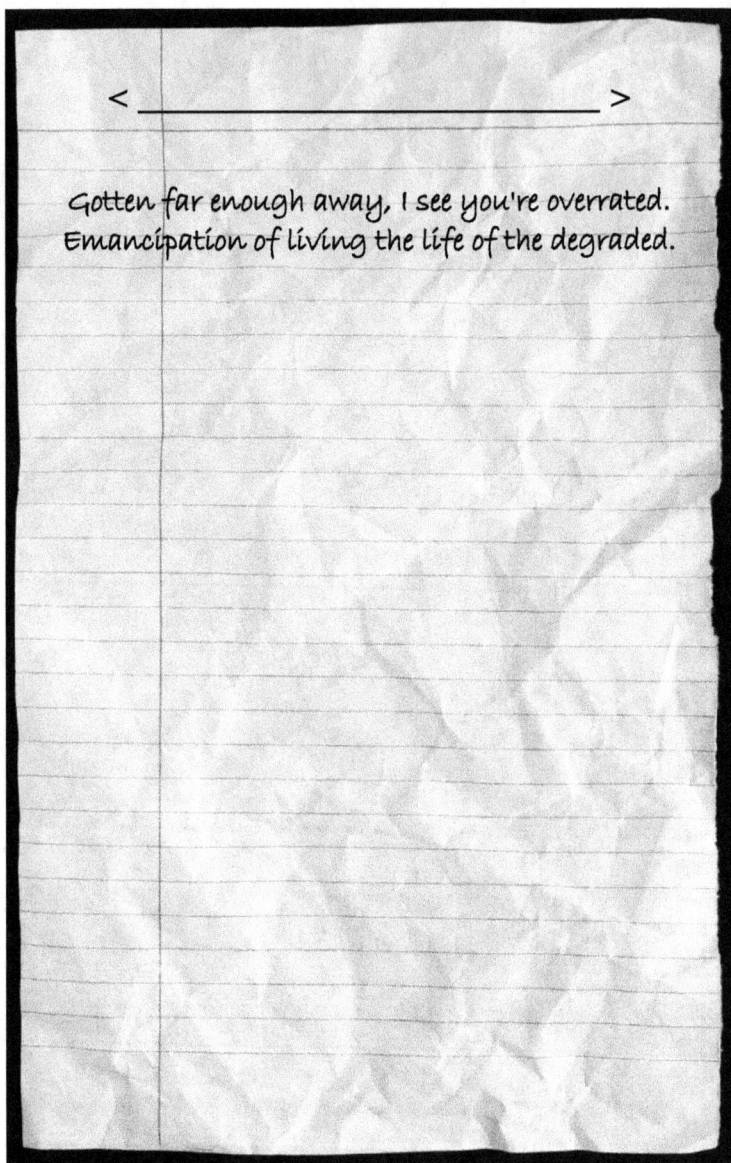

Gotten far enough away, I see you're overrated.
Emancipation of living the life of the degraded.

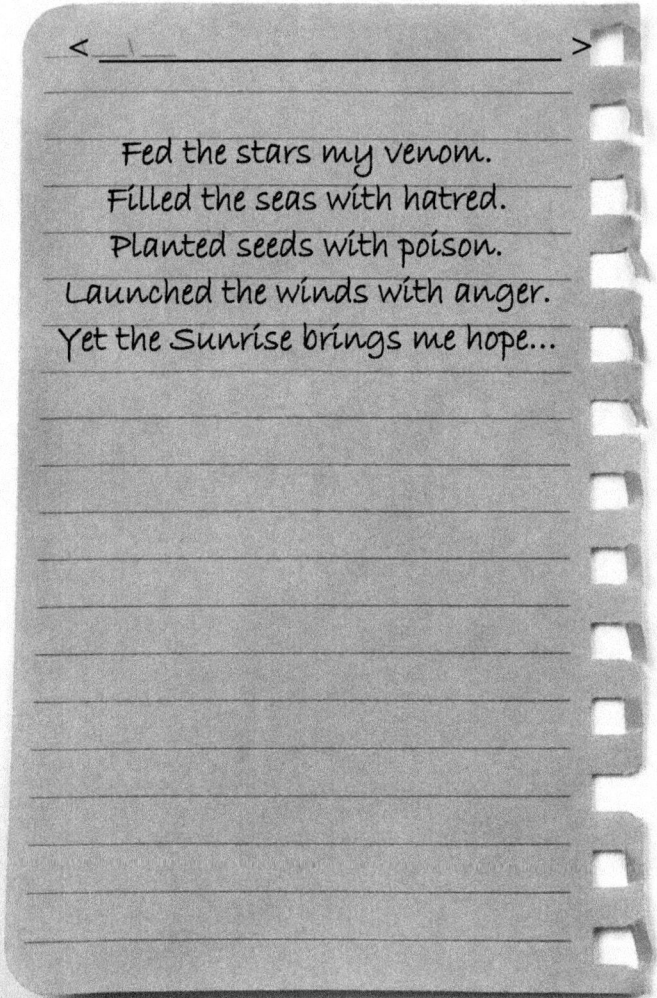

Fed the stars my venom.
Filled the seas with hatred.
Planted seeds with poison.
Launched the winds with anger.
Yet the Sunrise brings me hope...

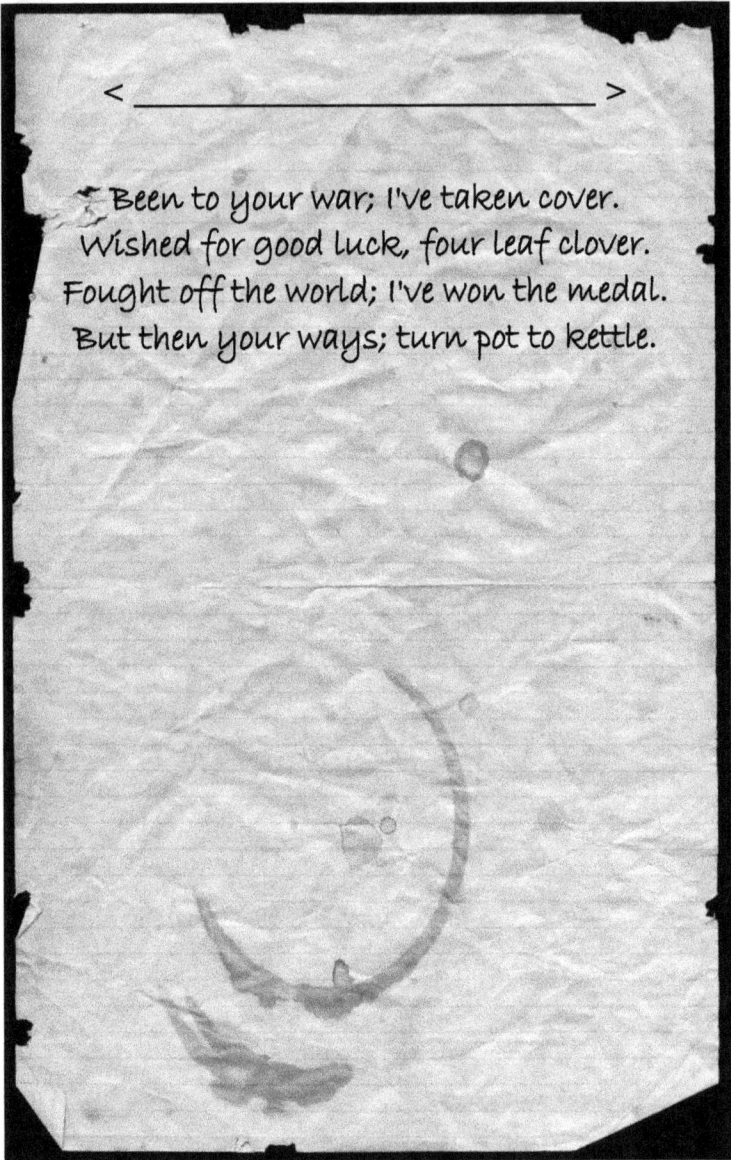

< _____ >

Been to your war; I've taken cover.
Wished for good luck, four leaf clover.
Fought off the world; I've won the medal.
But then your ways; turn pot to kettle.

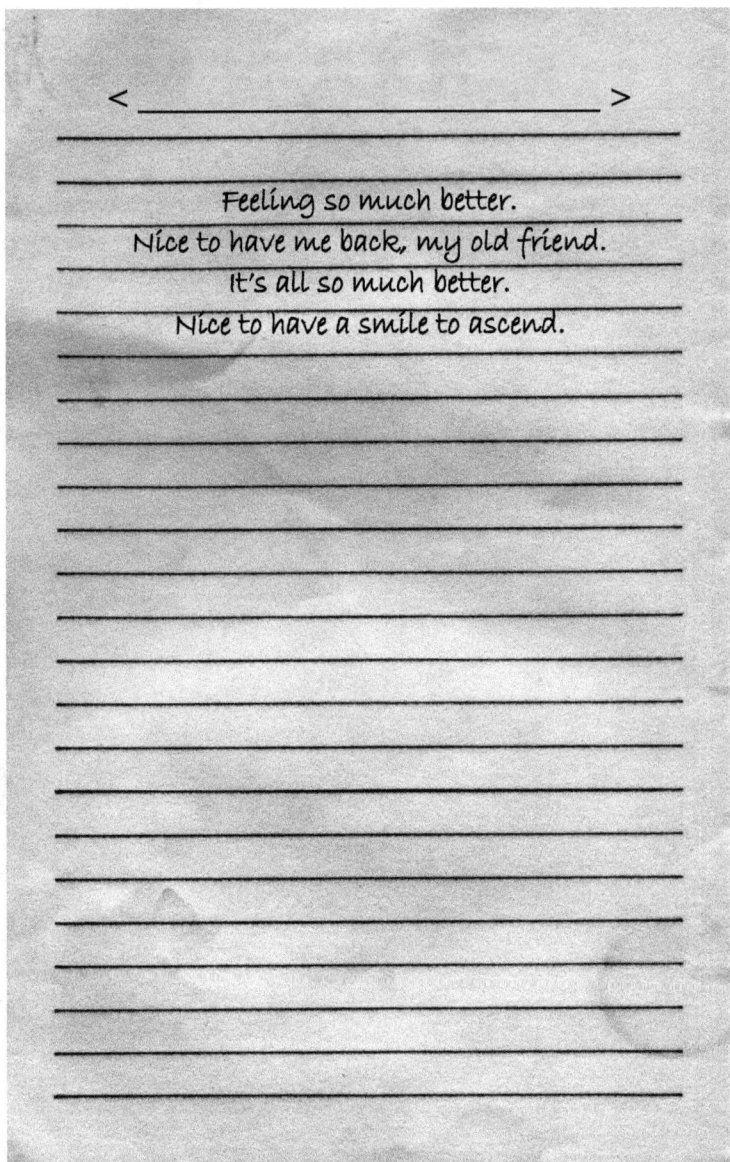

< _____ >

Feeling so much better.
Nice to have me back, my old friend.
It's all so much better.
Nice to have a smile to ascend.

< _____ >

Traffic lights glow red.
Buildings feel a little dead.
Streets may be bare.
Thinking this place is rare.
No other is home.
Always here after I roam.

< _____ >

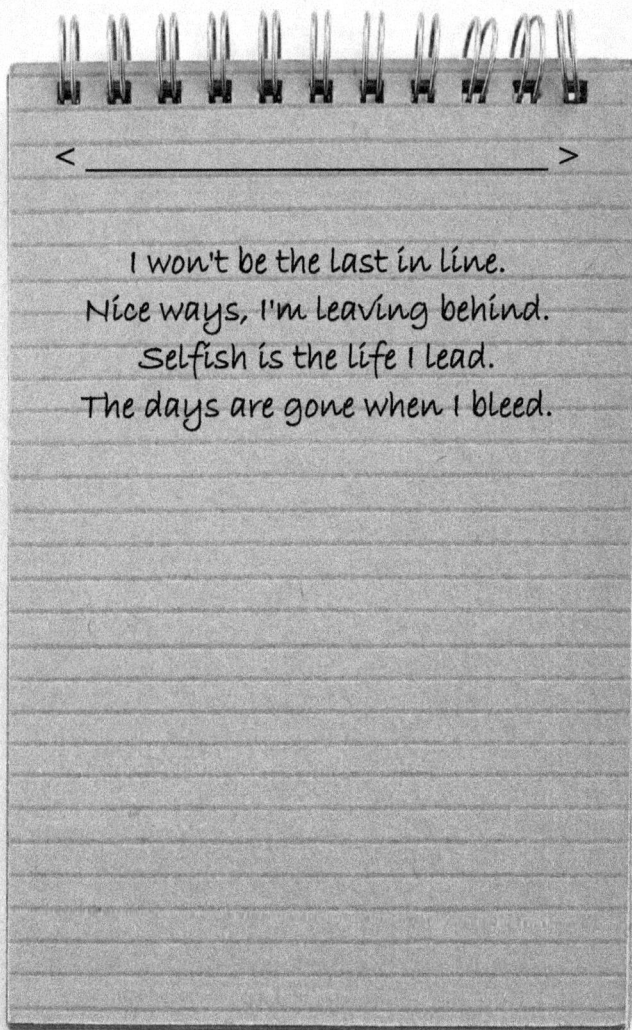

I won't be the last in line.
Nice ways, I'm leaving behind.
Selfish is the life I lead.
The days are gone when I bleed.

< _____ >

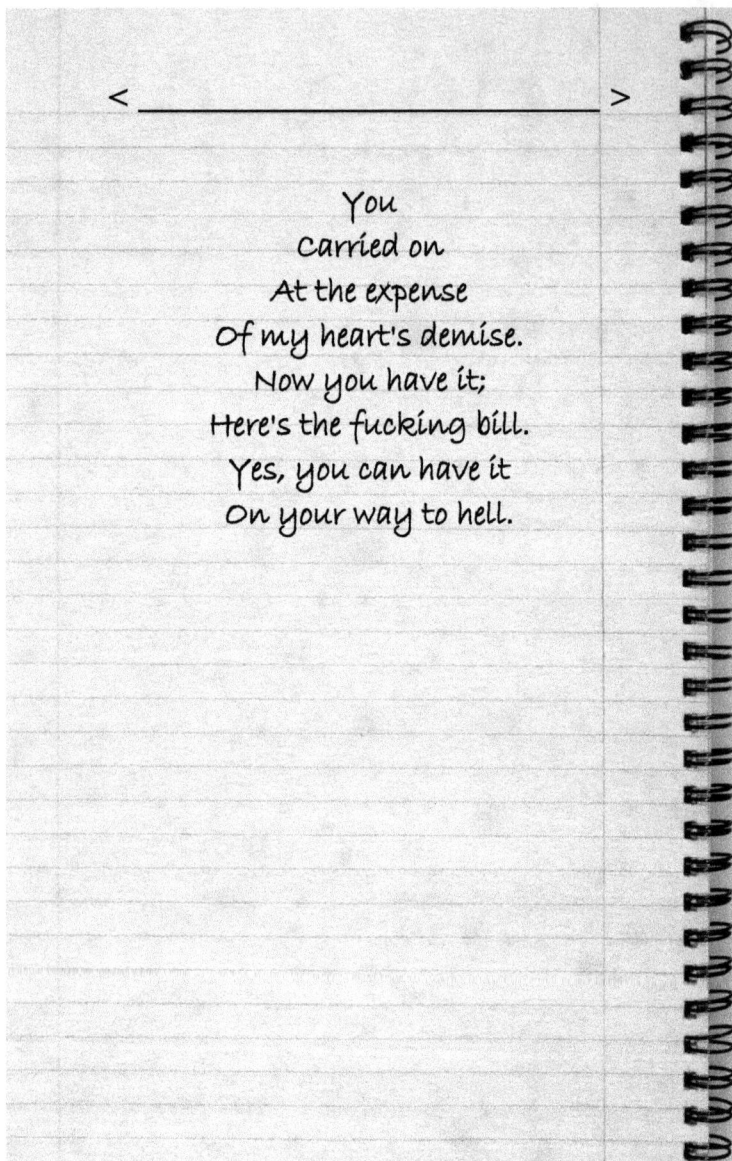

You
Carried on
At the expense
Of my heart's demise.
Now you have it;
Here's the fucking bill.
Yes, you can have it
On your way to hell.

< _____ >

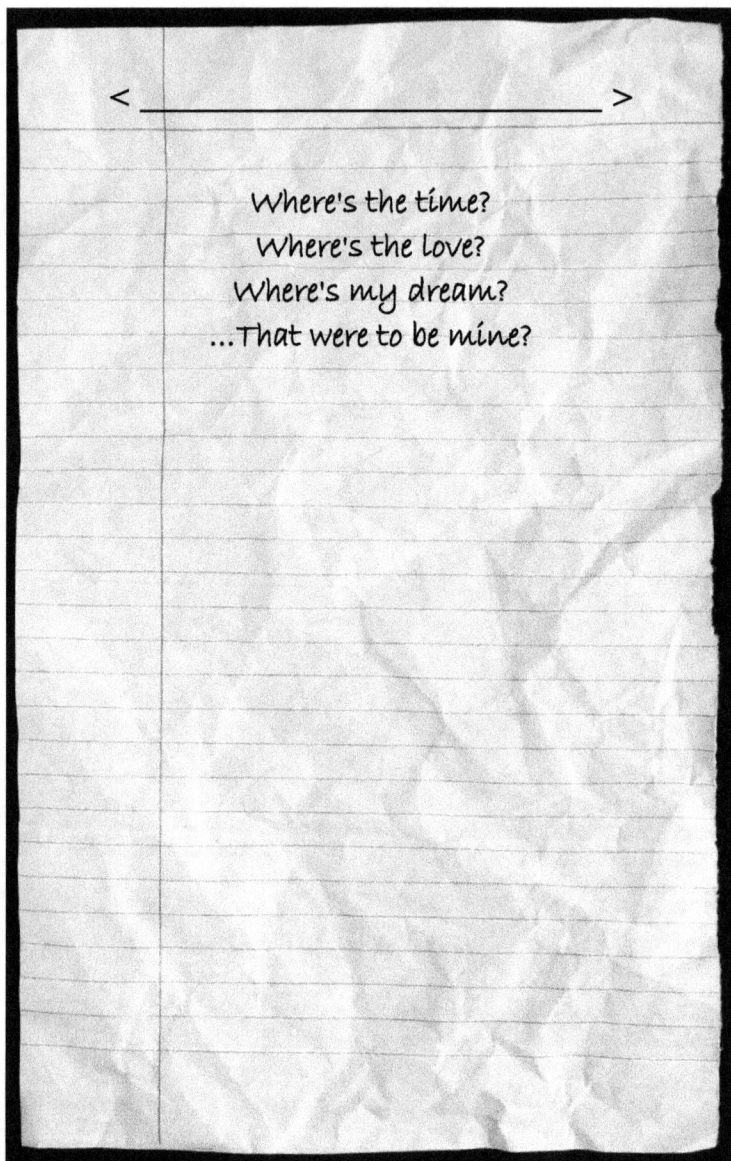

Where's the time?
Where's the love?
Where's my dream?
...That were to be mine?

< _____ >

I dream of a time coming soon
When I can follow you;
See the man you will be;
Watch the world through your eyes;
Aid you through failure;
Hear of your lessons learned;
Stand in your shadow, even more
proud of you;
Share stories of wild times;
Laugh at your wit and feel your
charm.

The ceiling isn't for walking.
The sky isn't for talking.
The ground isn't for swimming.
The tree isn't for trimming.
The door isn't for dinner.
The lie isn't the sinner.
The tear isn't for the whine.
The soul isn't for confine.
The world isn't for taking.
The heart isn't for breaking.

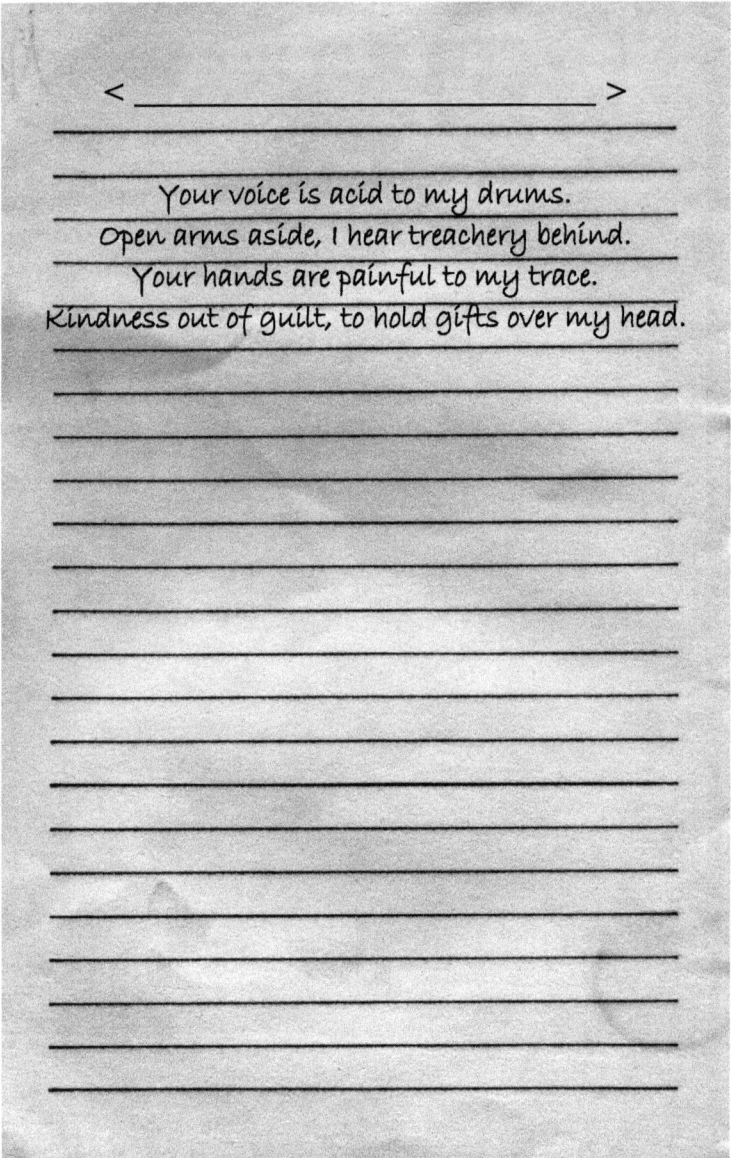

Your voice is acid to my drums.
Open arms aside, I hear treachery behind.
Your hands are painful to my trace.
Kindness out of guilt, to hold gifts over my head.

< _____ >

The road is full of pebbles.
Pebbles turn to mountains in your mind.
The path littered with troubles.
Troubles morph to breakdowns in your mind.
But don't worry, breathe slow; it's just fear.

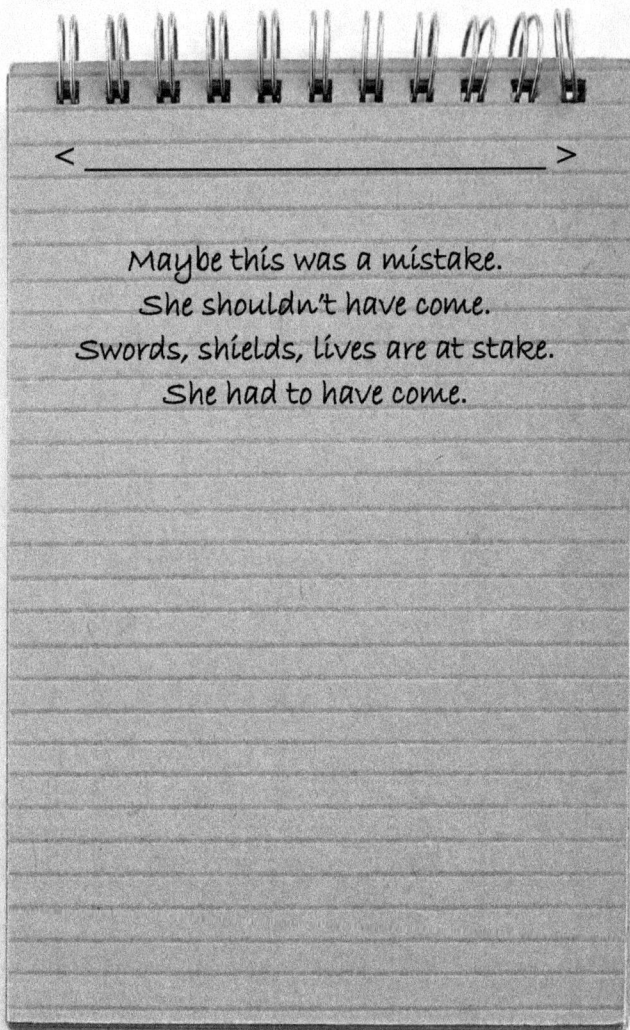

Maybe this was a mistake.
She shouldn't have come.
Swords, shields, lives are at stake.
She had to have come.

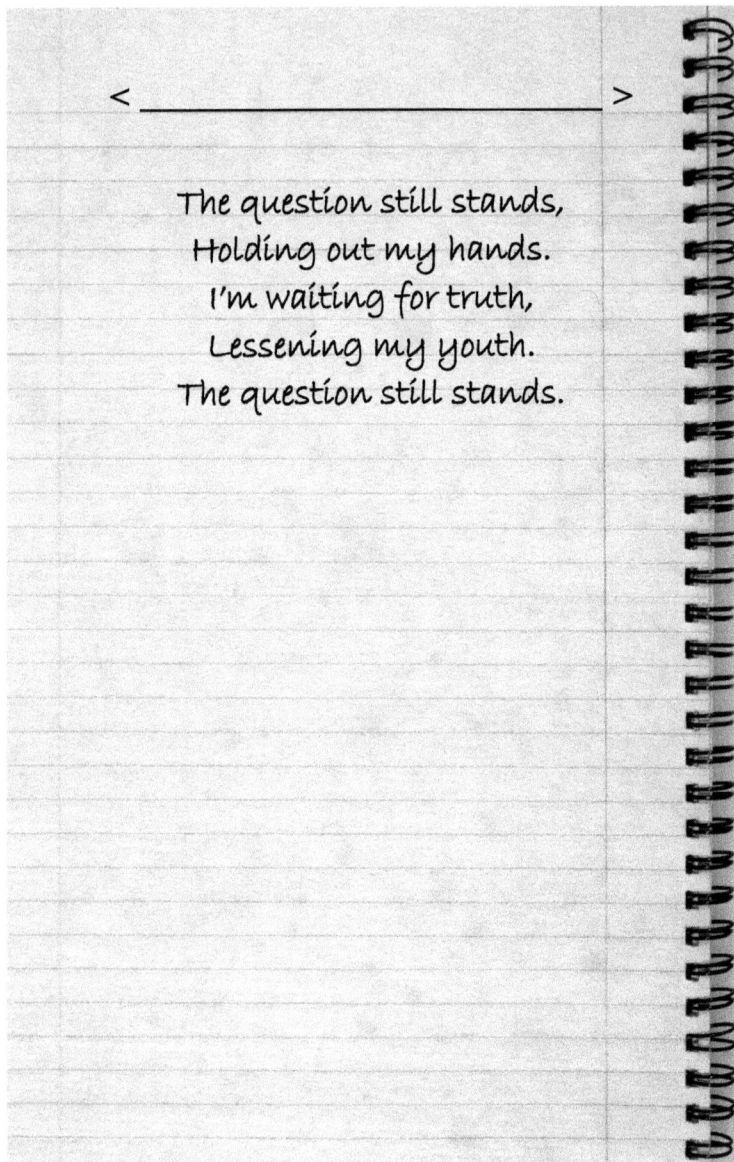

< _____ >

The question still stands,
Holding out my hands.
I'm waiting for truth,
Lessening my youth.
The question still stands.

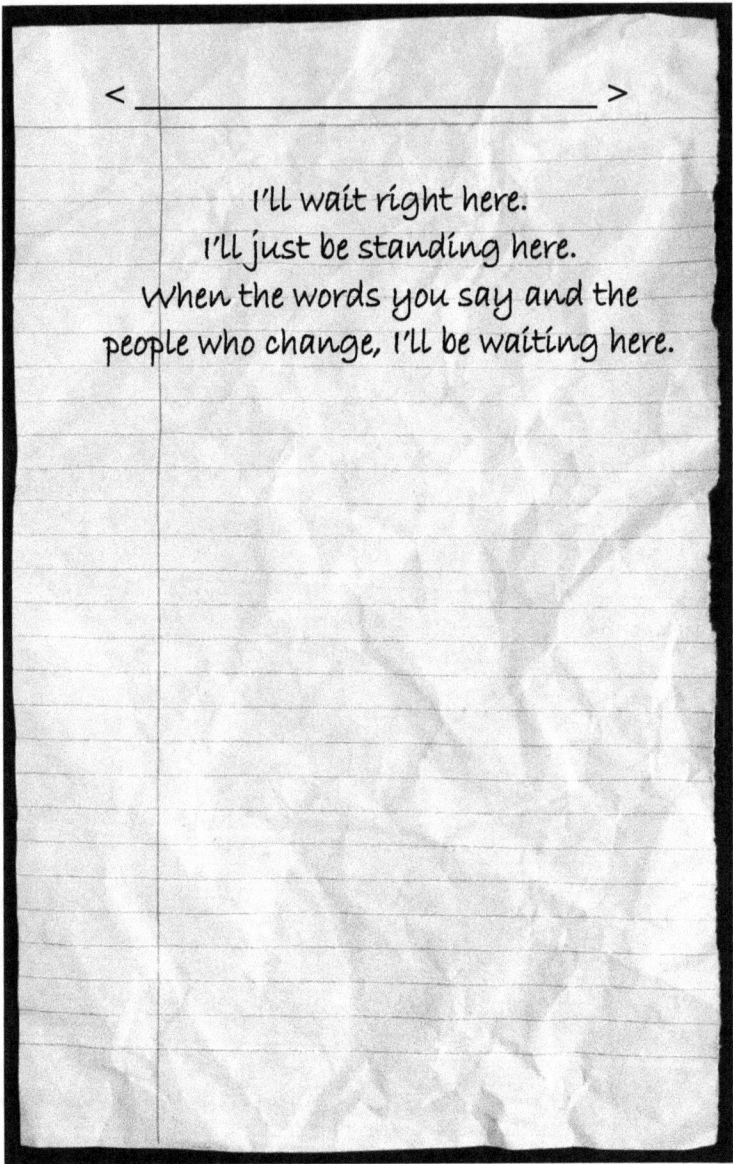

I'll wait right here.
I'll just be standing here.
When the words you say and the
people who change, I'll be waiting here.

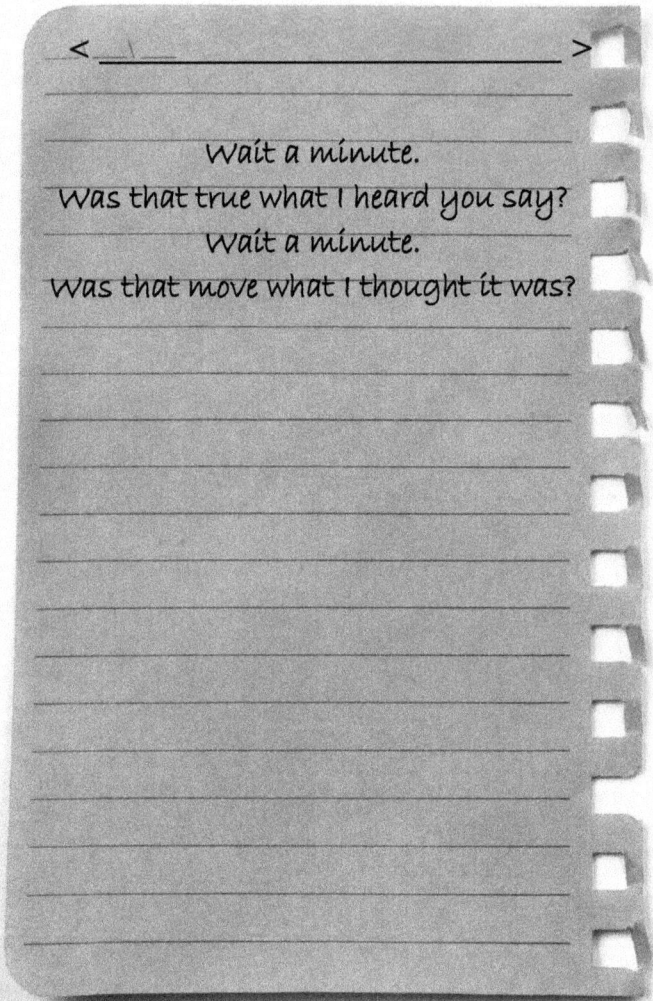

Wait a minute.
Was that true what I heard you say?
Wait a minute.
Was that move what I thought it was?

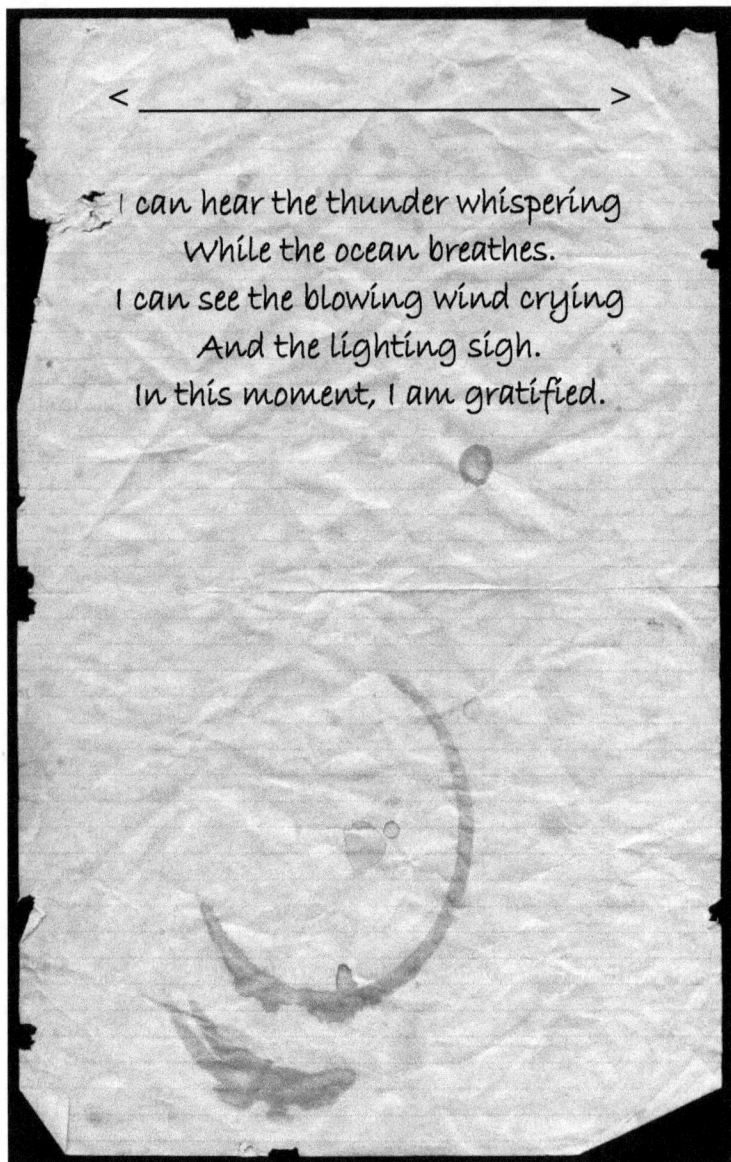

I can hear the thunder whispering
While the ocean breathes.
I can see the blowing wind crying
And the lighting sigh.
In this moment, I am gratified.

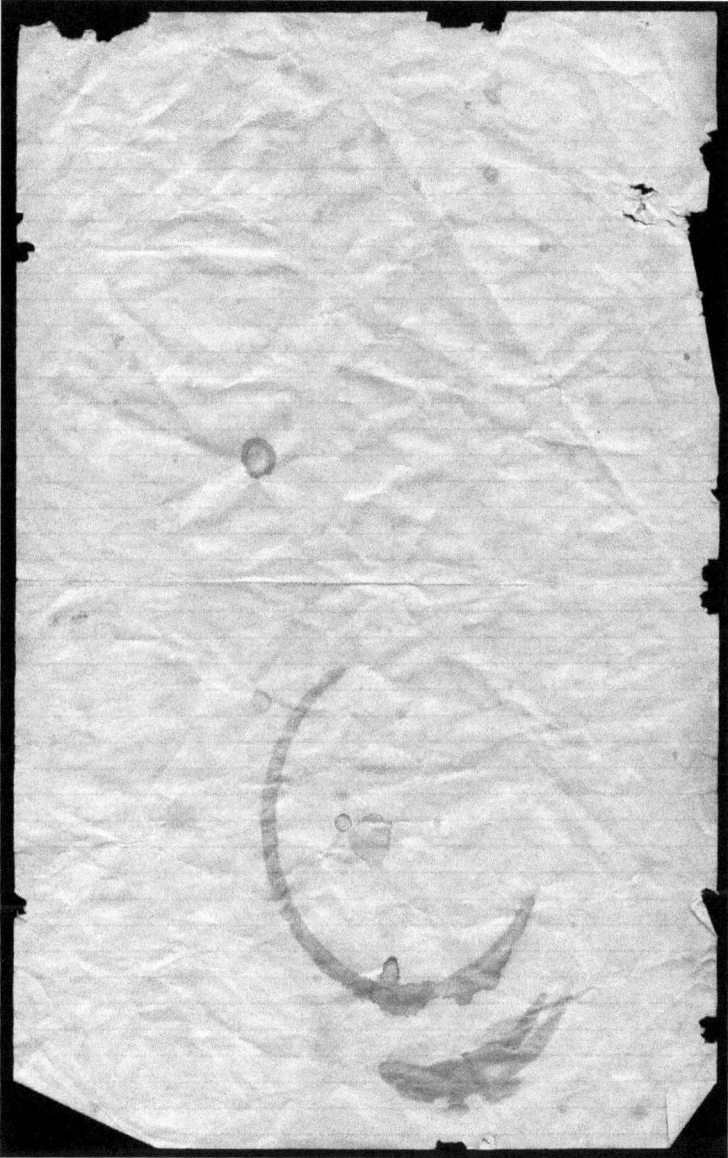

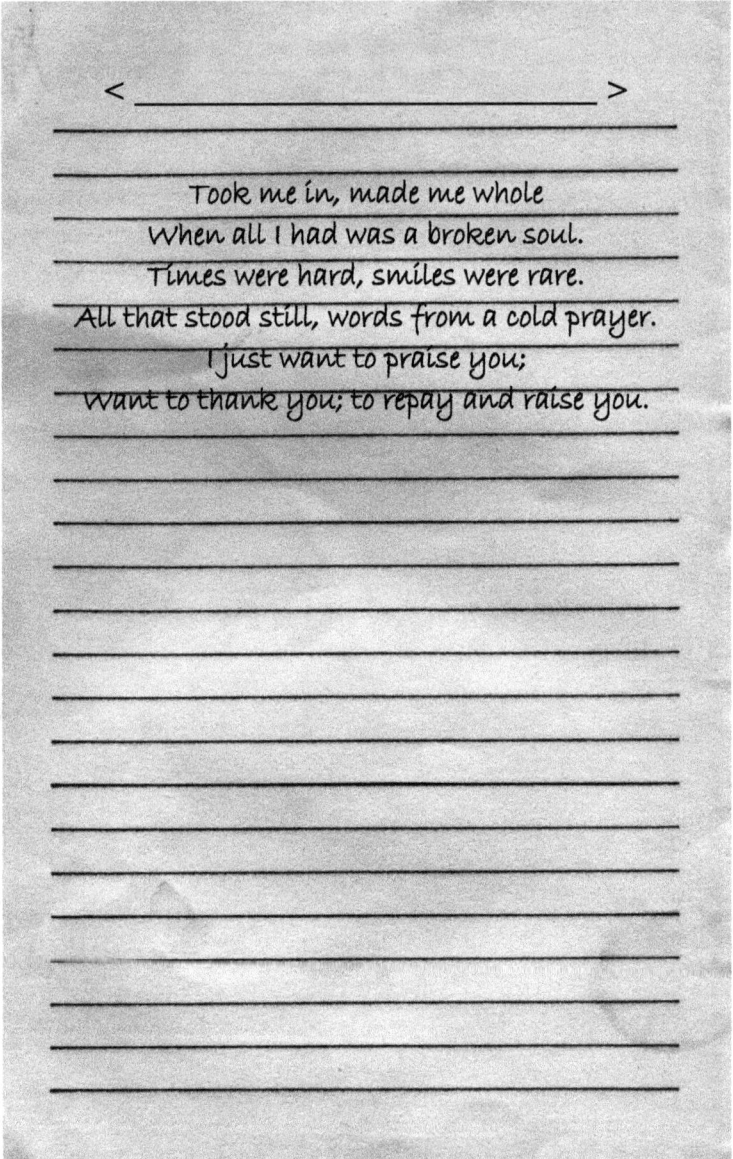

Took me in, made me whole
When all I had was a broken soul.
Times were hard, smiles were rare.
All that stood still, words from a cold prayer.
I just want to praise you;
Want to thank you; to repay and raise you.

< _____ >

Raining ashes on the other side.
Burning water in the ocean tide.
Are we all out of our fucking minds?
Colored towers in shades of maroon.
Washing babies with crystalized moon.
Are we all out of our fucking minds?
Singing praises to hate and despair.
Selling bridges to pay for stale air.
Are we all out of our fucking minds?
Eating kidneys to heal broken teeth.
Launching soldiers over baron heath.
Are we all out of our fucking minds?
Wasting treetops for the souls of breath.
Dancing circles, inviting Earth's death.
Are we out of our fucking minds?

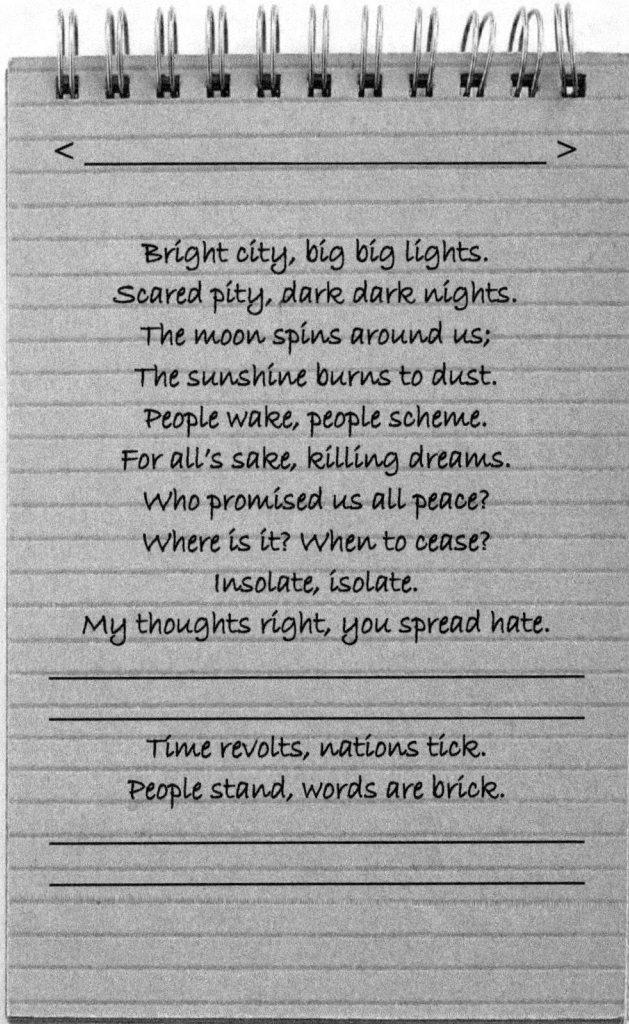

Bright city, big big lights.
Scared pity, dark dark nights.
The moon spins around us;
The sunshine burns to dust.
People wake, people scheme.
For all's sake, killing dreams.
Who promised us all peace?
Where is it? When to cease?
Insolate, isolate.
My thoughts right, you spread hate.

Time revolts, nations tick.
People stand, words are brick.

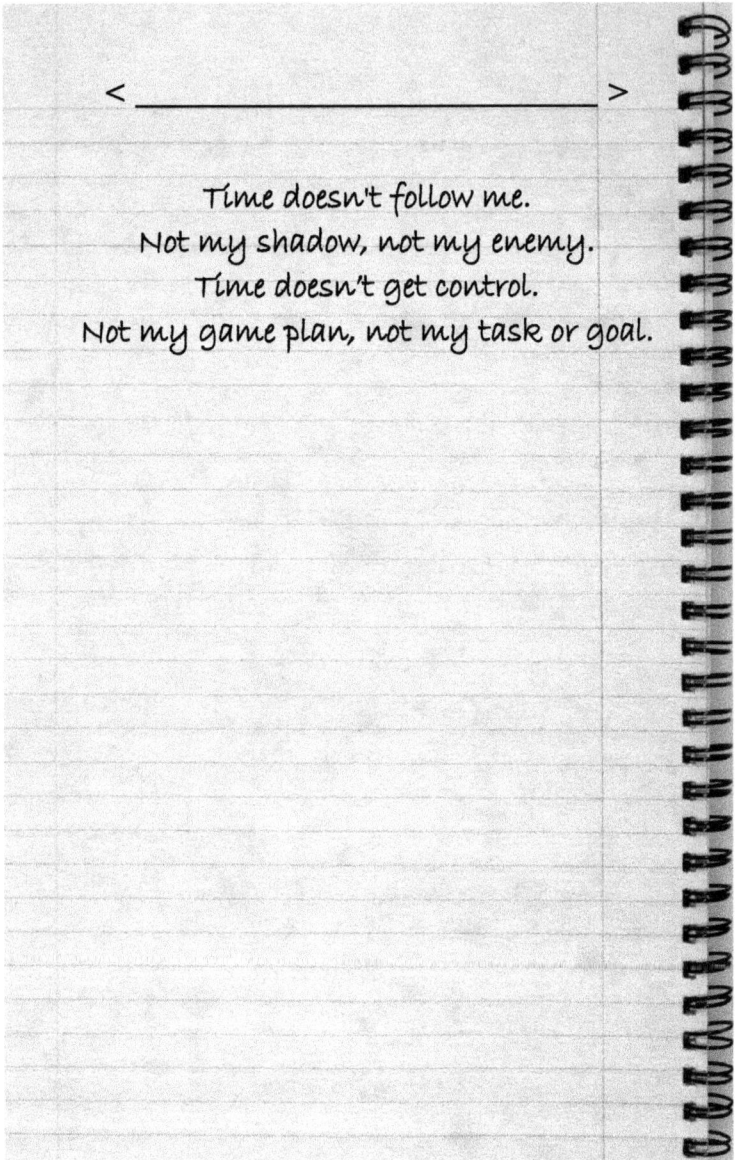

< _____ >

Time doesn't follow me.
Not my shadow, not my enemy.
Time doesn't get control.
Not my game plan, not my task or goal.

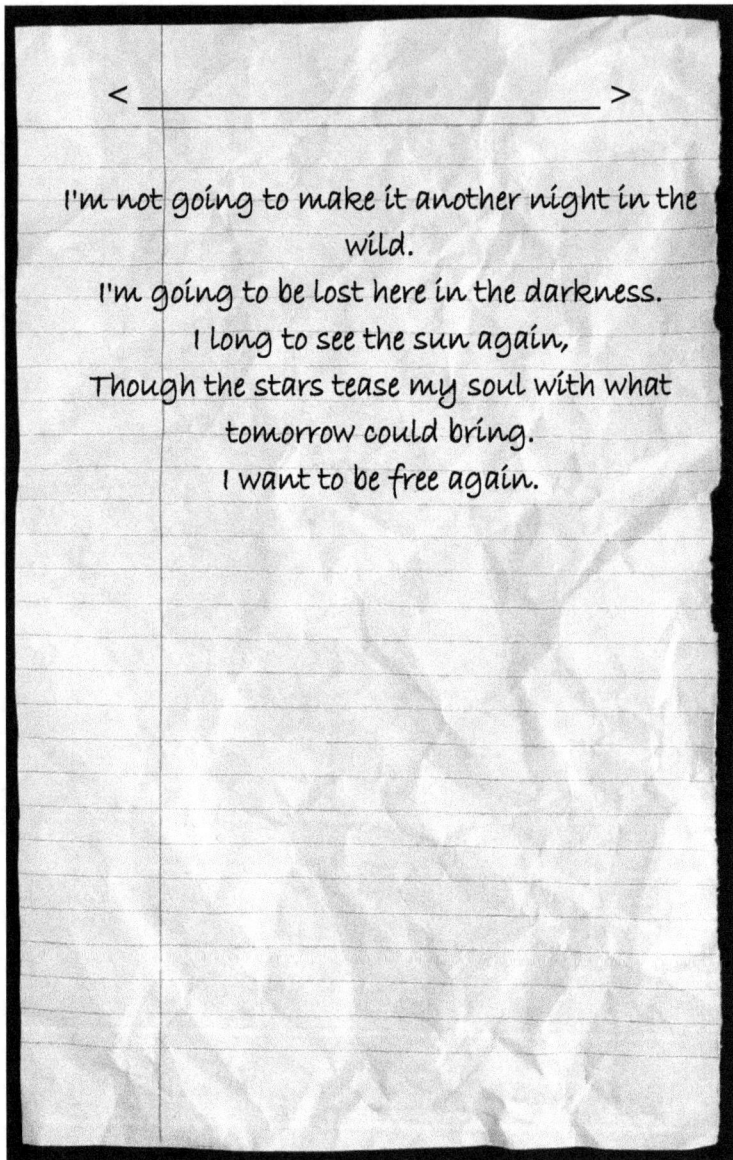

I'm not going to make it another night in the wild.
I'm going to be lost here in the darkness.
I long to see the sun again,
Though the stars tease my soul with what
tomorrow could bring.
I want to be free again.

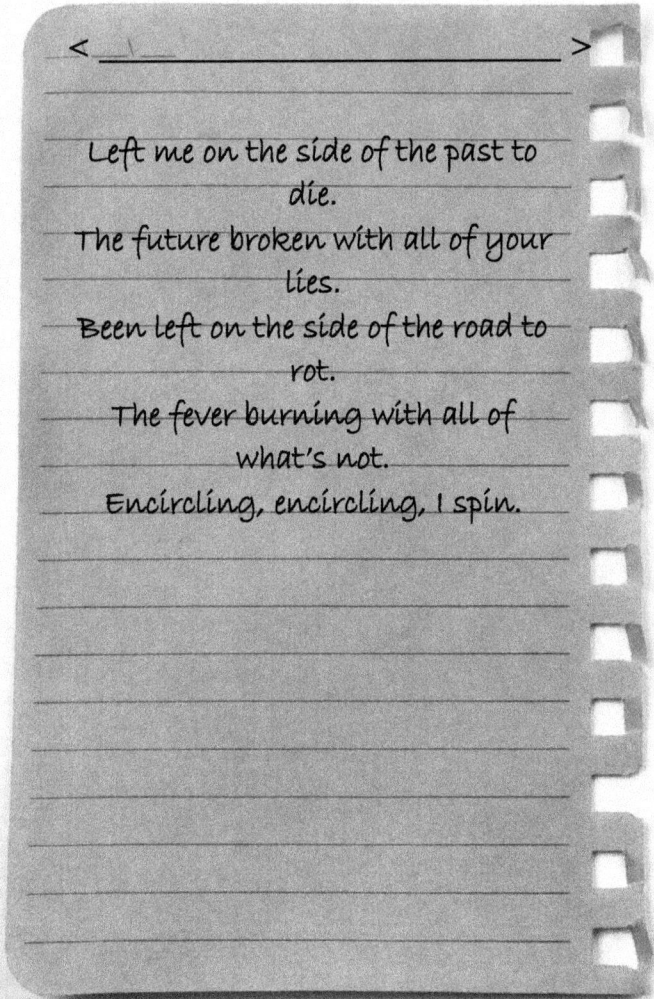

< _____ >

Left me on the side of the past to
die.
The future broken with all of your
lies.
Been left on the side of the road to
rot.
The fever burning with all of
what's not.
Encircling, encircling, I spin.

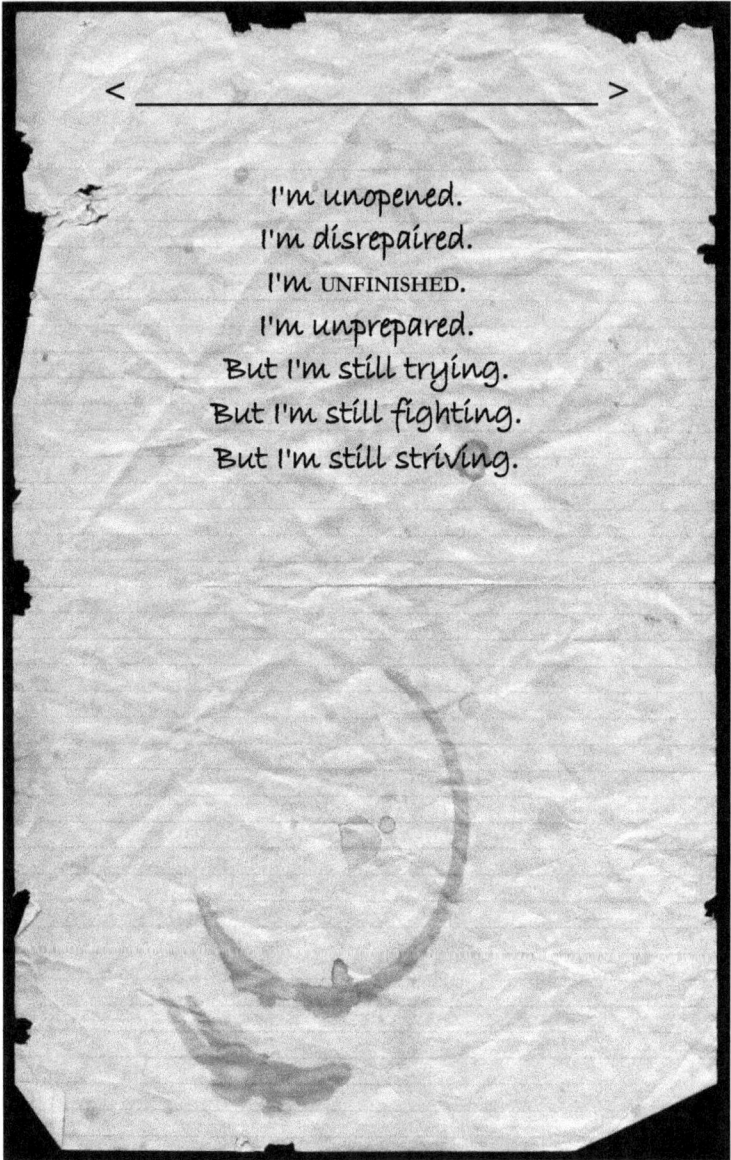

I'm unopened.
I'm disrepaired.
I'm UNFINISHED.
I'm unprepared.
But I'm still trying.
But I'm still fighting.
But I'm still striving.

< _____ >

He feels bayed by the dogs.
The darkness slowly closing in.
Lost in a thousand fogs.
The growls near, snoots nosing in.
Hairs rise, adrenal eyes search.
~~Find none, yet fevered breath is near.~~
~~Amused, Lucifer watches, perched.~~
~~Laughing, knowing his beasts smell fear.~~

< _____ >

Hot in imagination.
Creative energies abuzz, surrounds.
Mind screams in rare reflection,
Letting subconscious wage war and surmount.
Time and place and love and hate;
Good and evil in worlds that I create;
Young and old and girl and boy;
Games and plots, and the subtext they employ;
Simple truths and complex lies;
Wrapped up morals in laughs and in cries;
Exhausted exuberance;
Yet left with renewed life in touch with souls;
The results protuberance;
Then a new journey repeats: grows, crafts, molds.

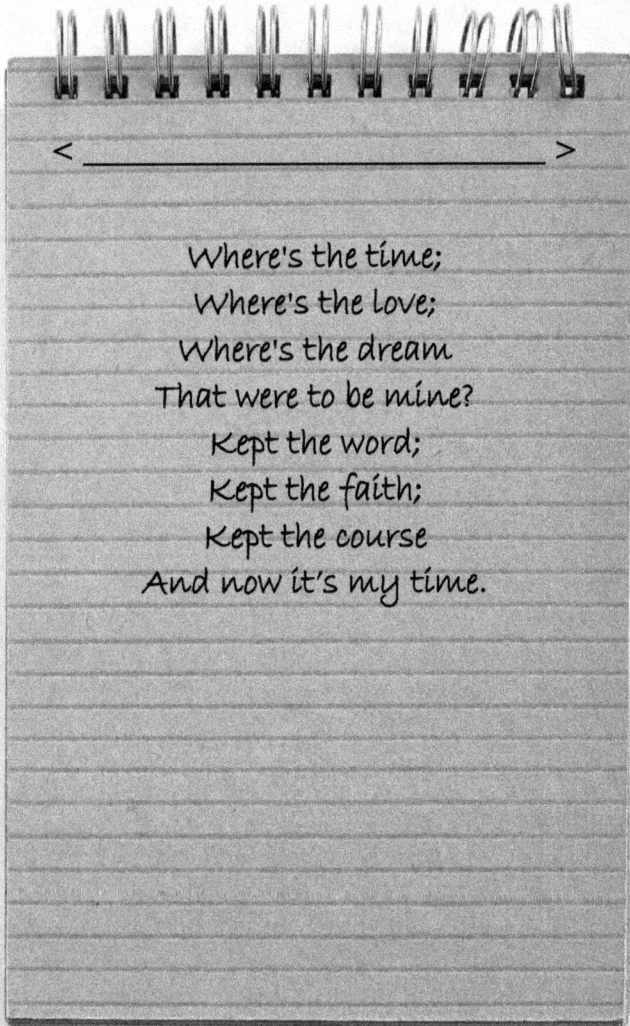

Where's the time;
Where's the love;
Where's the dream
That were to be mine?
Kept the word;
Kept the faith;
Kept the course
And now it's my time.

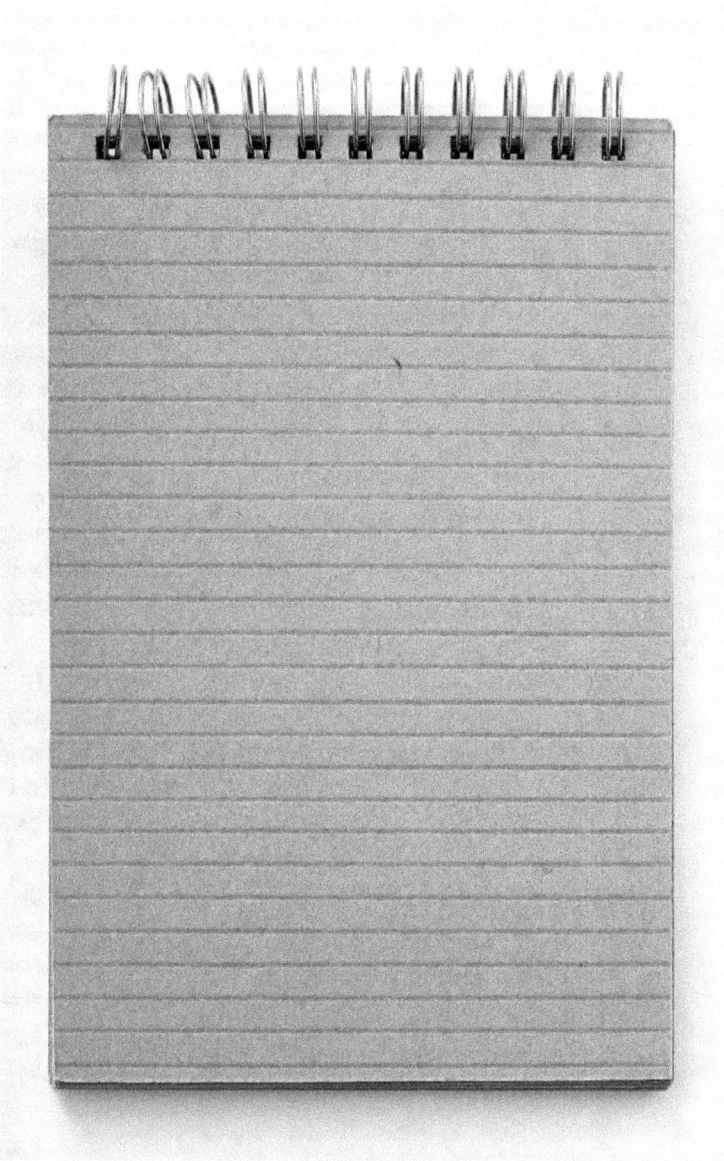

< _____ >

I can see it coming;
Momentum building.
The rage and the motion;
Moment so thrilling.
I can feel it crashing,
Twisting, and curling.
Its teeth holding, gnashing,
Powerful whirling.
Free from its deadly cage.
Left again, I'm awed.
Charge back into the rage
Just to feel a god.

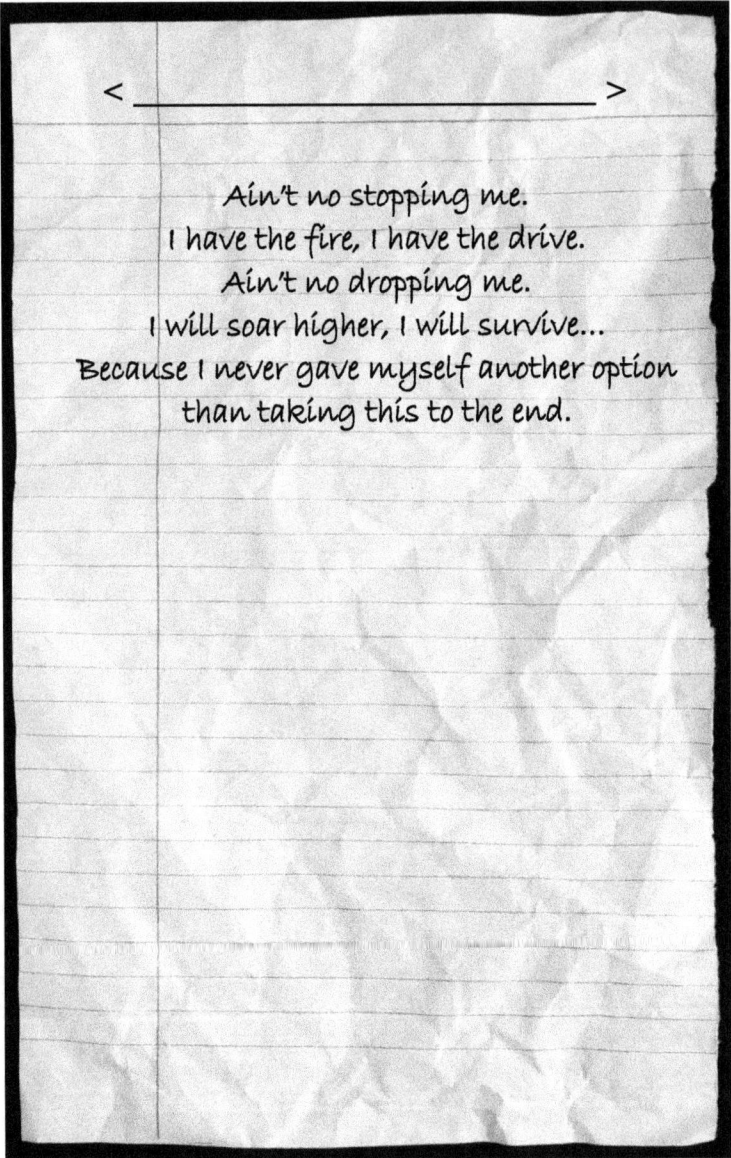

Ain't no stopping me.
I have the fire, I have the drive.
Ain't no dropping me.
I will soar higher, I will survive...
Because I never gave myself another option
than taking this to the end.

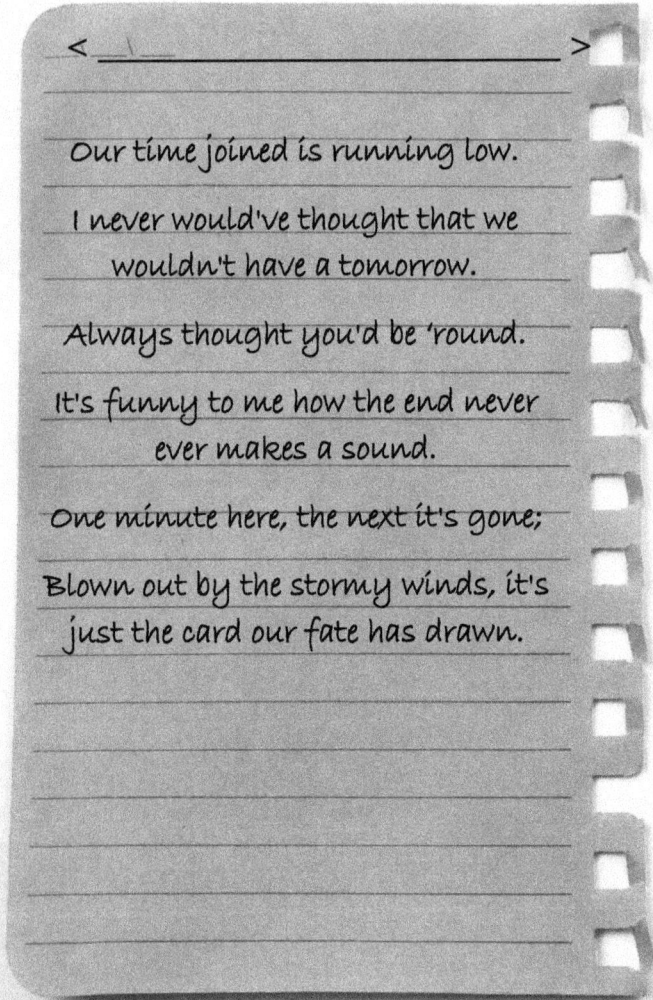

Our time joined is running low.

I never would've thought that we
wouldn't have a tomorrow.

Always thought you'd be 'round.

It's funny to me how the end never
ever makes a sound.

One minute here, the next it's gone;

Blown out by the stormy winds, it's
just the card our fate has drawn.

< _____ >

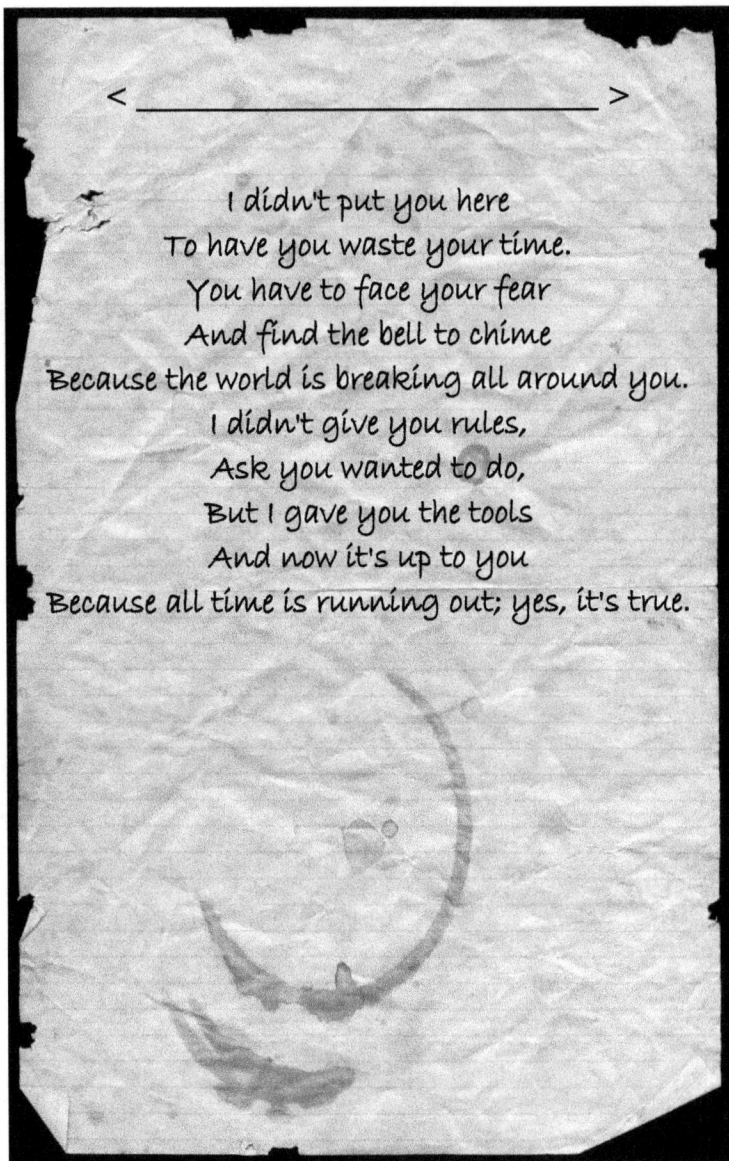

I didn't put you here
To have you waste your time.
You have to face your fear
And find the bell to chime
Because the world is breaking all around you.
I didn't give you rules,
Ask you wanted to do,
But I gave you the tools
And now it's up to you
Because all time is running out; yes, it's true.

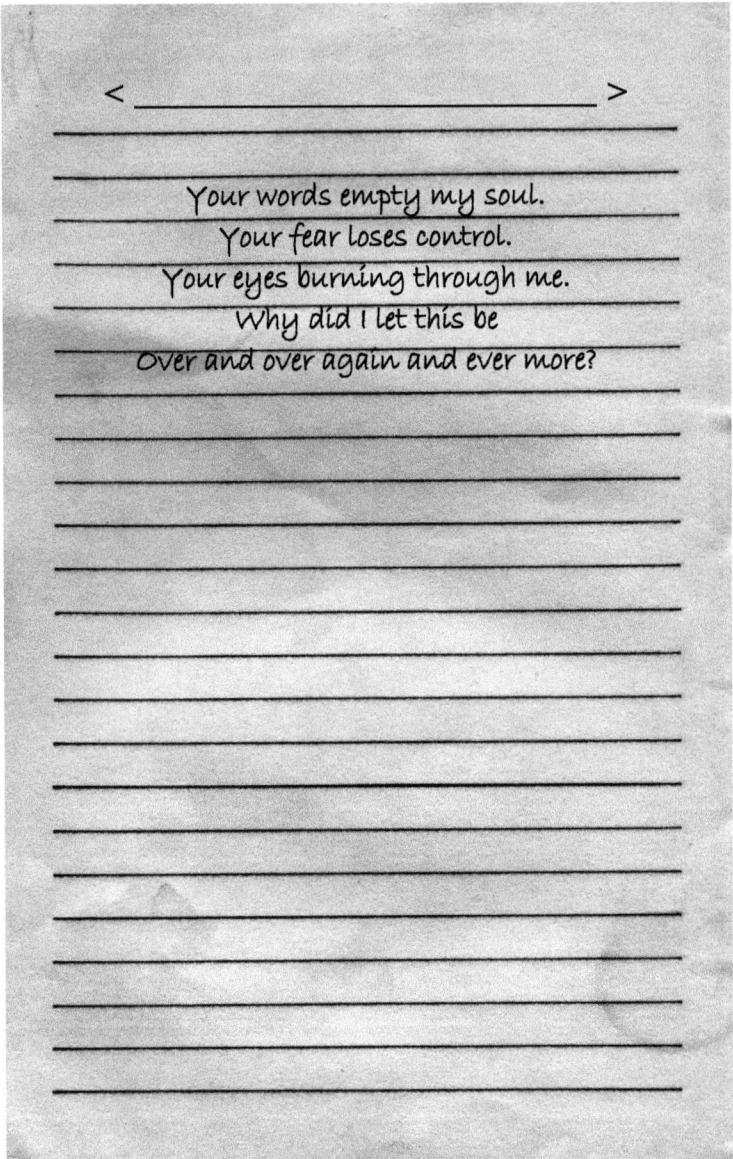

< _____ >

Your words empty my soul.
Your fear loses control.
Your eyes burning through me.
Why did I let this be
Over and over again and ever more?

< _____ >

Lay cloth across time.
Blind it from knowing.
Keep its hands from climb;
Moments I'm stowing.

< _____ >

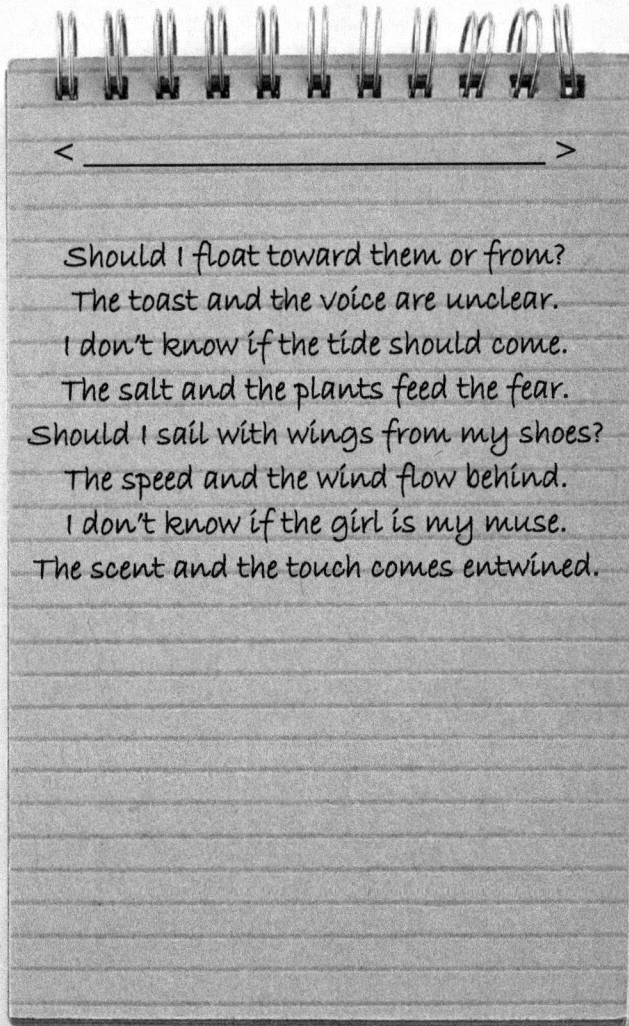

Should I float toward them or from?
The toast and the voice are unclear.
I don't know if the tide should come.
The salt and the plants feed the fear.
Should I sail with wings from my shoes?
The speed and the wind flow behind.
I don't know if the girl is my muse.
The scent and the touch comes entwined.

< _____ >

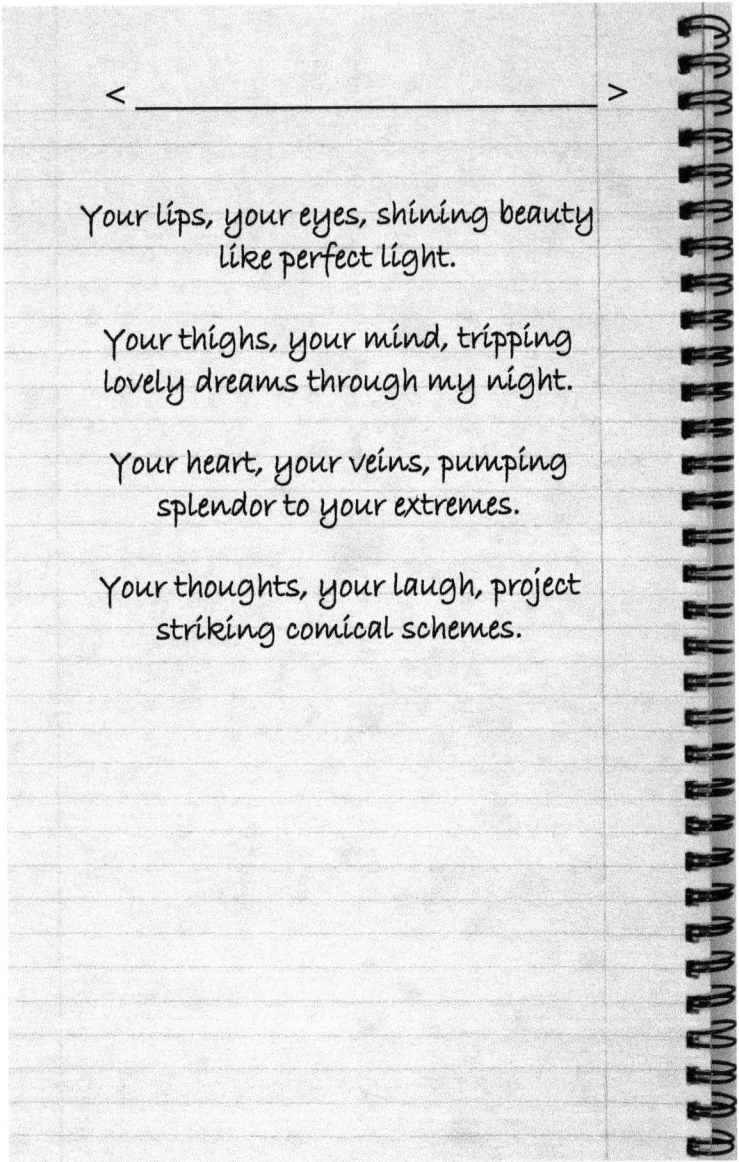

Your lips, your eyes, shining beauty
like perfect light.

Your thighs, your mind, tripping
lovely dreams through my night.

Your heart, your veins, pumping
splendor to your extremes.

Your thoughts, your laugh, project
striking comical schemes.

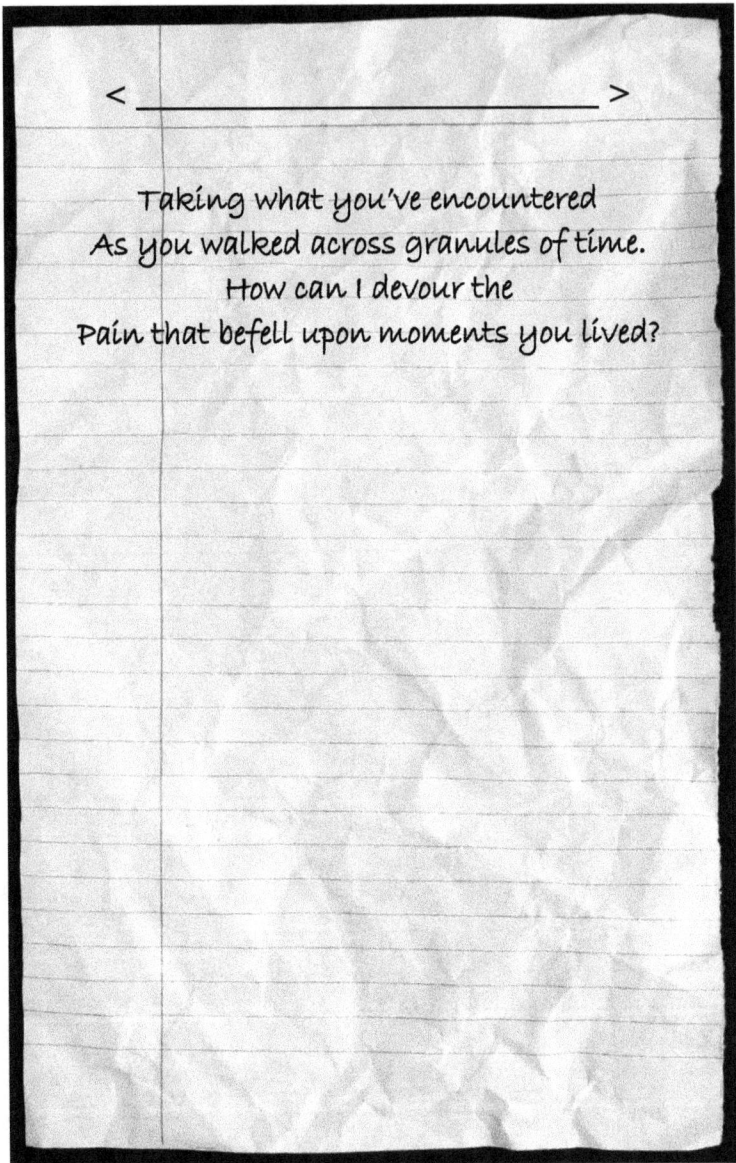

Taking what you've encountered
As you walked across granules of time.
How can I devour the
Pain that befell upon moments you lived?

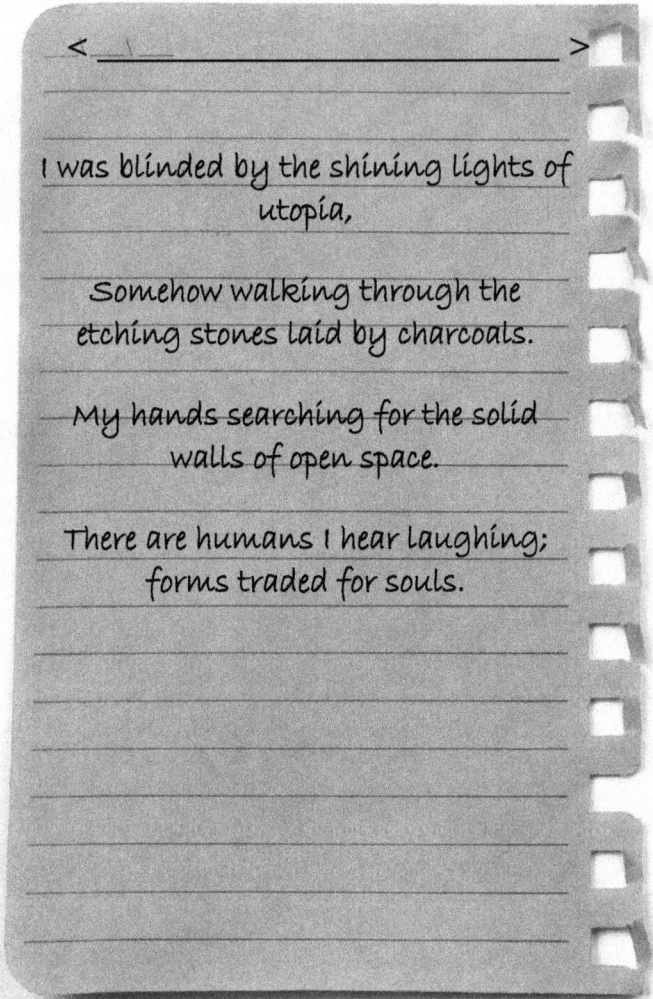

< _____ >

I was blinded by the shining lights of utopia,

Somehow walking through the etching stones laid by charcoals.

My hands searching for the solid walls of open space.

There are humans I hear laughing; forms traded for souls.

< ———————————————— >

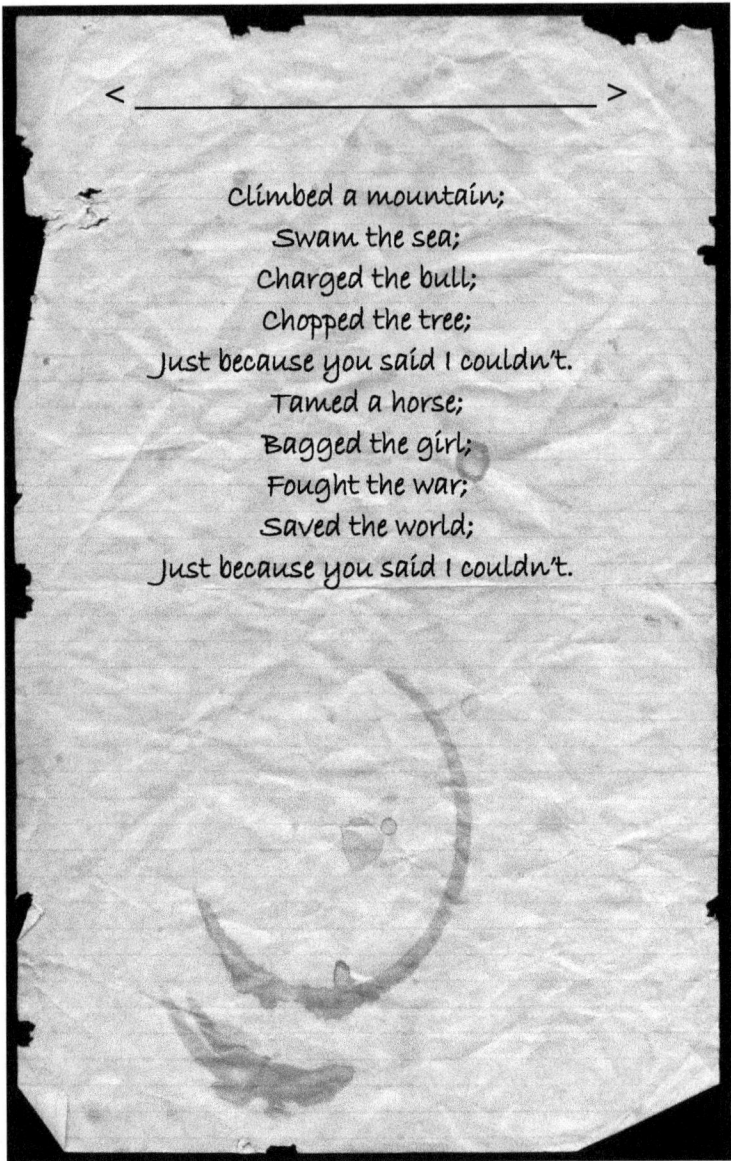

Climbed a mountain;
Swam the sea;
Charged the bull;
Chopped the tree;
Just because you said I couldn't.
Tamed a horse;
Bagged the girl;
Fought the war;
Saved the world;
Just because you said I couldn't.

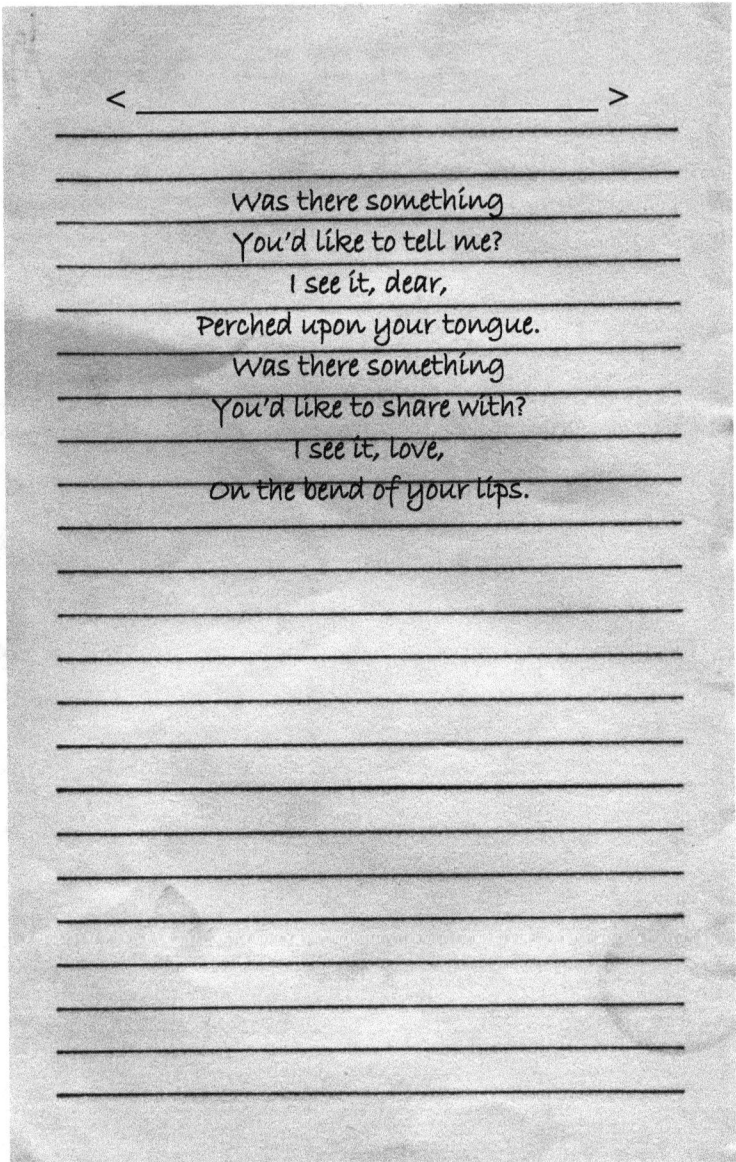

Was there something
You'd like to tell me?
I see it, dear,
Perched upon your tongue.
Was there something
You'd like to share with?
I see it, love,
On the bend of your lips.

About Chris Wendel

Chris Wendel is an Amazon.com bestselling author for his short story, *Human After All: The Pen Pal Chronicle*. The short story chronicles the teen years of the villain in his debut novel, *Human After All*, which introduced characters Det. Tom Gray and Valerie Hardy. The follow-up novel, *King of Pain*, featuring Det. Tom Gray will be released at the end of 2013. In the summer of 2013, Chris's business book *Converting Customers to Clients* was released. Also in the summer of 2013, Chris published *On Strengthening Business Relationships* is a book of standalone business quotes.

He is currently available for book club engagements, organizational presentations for both his creative writing and client relationship/customer service topics. He blogs at his web site cwendel.com about various topics, which include arts and entertainment, business, customer service, writing, music, parenting, and more.

Chris is involved in numerous community activities and groups, like Kiwanis and the local futbol club. Chris enjoys football, soccer, music, stories and reading, as well as spending precious time with friends and family.

www.cwendel.com